Ancient Egypt

Ancient Egypt

Art, architecture and history

Francesco Tiradritti

THE BRITISH MUSEUM PRESS

How to use this book

For ease of use, this book is divided into three main themes, identified by the coloured bands on the sides of the pages. Yellow stands for 'art and architecture', blue for 'historical and cultural context', and pink for 'great masterpieces'. Each double-page spread deals with a specific subject and comprises an introduction, illustrations and commentary on the illustrations. The book can therefore be read in sequence or according to the reader's own particular areas of interest. The appendices include maps, a chronology, an index of historical names and divinities, and further details of the main museums mentioned in the text.

Frontispiece:
The goddesses Nephthys and Isis and a figure of the god Osiris-Ra, from the tomb of Nefertari.

Contents

4000-2065 BC

2065-1550 BC

1550-1075 BC

1075-30 BC

Midday

Twilight

Appendices

How to read Egyptian art

There were two main forms of artistic expression in ancient Egypt: sculpture and relief. Painting was not an art form in its own right, but was used to complement two-dimensional representations.

Much of the sculpture was designed to be viewed from the front; this is apparent in the very earliest statues, which make no real attempt at three-dimensional representation. Later on, as a result of the belief that figures were not just representations of people but actually replacements for them, volume was treated in a more realistic manner. Profile poses became more common from the late Old Kingdom onwards, and three-quarter views were occasionally used.

Statues tended to be made in shapes which fitted inside geometric figures, in an attempt to keep the block of stone as intact as possible. There was therefore a preference for statuary in which surfaces were modelled in an abstract way.

Two-dimensional representation breaks down reality into two planes and seeks to reproduce every aspect of it in an immediately recognizable manner, so the human figure was shown in a compromise between a frontal view focusing on the eyes, ears and chest, and a side view showing the head, torso and limbs. Figures were arranged in an ordered, symmetrical manner within the available space, and images were divided into rows, or registers, with the figures standing on the bottom line. The figures could break through the baseline to give a sense of depth and perspective to the scene, or the baseline could be reshaped to suggest spatial features such as deserts or hills.

Hieroglyphic writing was used as an integral part of decoration, and figures could be depicted so that they resembled script. This intermingling of art forms also included architecture, since buildings were a medium for art, units of meaning in their own right which were designed not only to be seen, but to be read and interpreted.

Statue of the vizier Hemiunu, Hildesheim, Pelizaeus Museum, 1962. This 4th-dynasty masterpiece shows a completely frontal view of the human figure which, although it complies with abstract laws of geometry, still leaves plenty of room for the artist's sensitivity to be expressed.

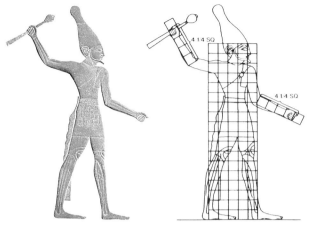

◄ The human figure was always created using a grid pattern, so the figures in a scene were of uniform size. Here, a detail from the palette of King Narmer (see p. 16) has been broken down into its constituent parts (Iversen, *Canon and proportions in Egyptian art*, Warminster 1975, table 15). This shows how artists had not yet developed a canon, or rule, as to how the human figure should be subdivided.

◄ *Painted relief depicting King Horemheb and the goddess Isis, from Horemheb's tomb in the Valley of the Kings* (KV 57). The male and female figures are shown using different conventions, which highlight not only the anatomical differences between them but also their roles in society. Men are normally shown walking and women standing, to signify the more active role played by men. Women traditionally have pale skin, reflecting their largely indoor, domestic existence, whereas men have brick-red complexions as a result of working outdoors.

Time and movement in Egyptian art

Official works of Egyptian art, in other words those intended to glorify and perpetuate the image of a king or god, complied with a series of rules known as canons. Sculptures and reliefs were made by workshops rather than individuals, and therefore convey the artistic sensibilities of their time as opposed to those of one individual.

This was not so much the case with works that were not intended for public consumption, but were made for a restricted circle of people or for the artist that produced them. True individual artistry, often of an extremely high standard, is apparent in scenes from everyday life depicted in the tombs of ordinary people, quick sketches and drawings on ostraca (limestone flakes or potsherds), and the decoration of everyday objects. These works display a sense of freedom and experimentation which is only rarely apparent in official statues and reliefs. Rather than working to a pre-existing model, the artist aims to reproduce reality as vividly as possible using the resources available. In this quest, time and movement play a fundamental role.

◀ ▼ *Rural scene from the tomb of Unsu,* Paris, Musée du Louvre, N 1431 (18th dynasty). It reads upwards from the bottom. Each register shows one aspect of cultivation - sowing and harvesting. These activities are shown in sequence with no indication of continuity, as in Giorgione's painting *The three ages of man* (Florence, Palazzo Pitti), where the passing of time is shown by the ages of the three figures. The boy in the centre implies that the picture is meant to be read in circular fashion, suggesting the cyclical nature of existence.

▶ *Disc from the tomb of Hemaka*, Cairo, Egyptian Museum, JE 70164 (1st dynasty). To Egyptian artists, movement and the passing of time are shown by depicting figures side by side. A jackal (with the different colours simply indicating the existence of different types of the same animal) is shown chasing and attacking a small herbivore, with the emphasis on the two key moments of the hunt. The sense of motion is conveyed by the circular form of the object.

This method is based on close observation of nature, and is similar to the first studies of movement in Eadweard James Muybridge's *Animal locomotion* (Paris 1887, Cinémathèque Française, plate 739).

▶ Gianni De Luca's famous comic book *Il commissario Spada* uses the Egyptian technique of reproducing time and movement by breaking down an action into stages. The scenes are linked by the head of the commissioner, which increasingly breaks through the dividing line between them and overlaps with the previous picture.

9

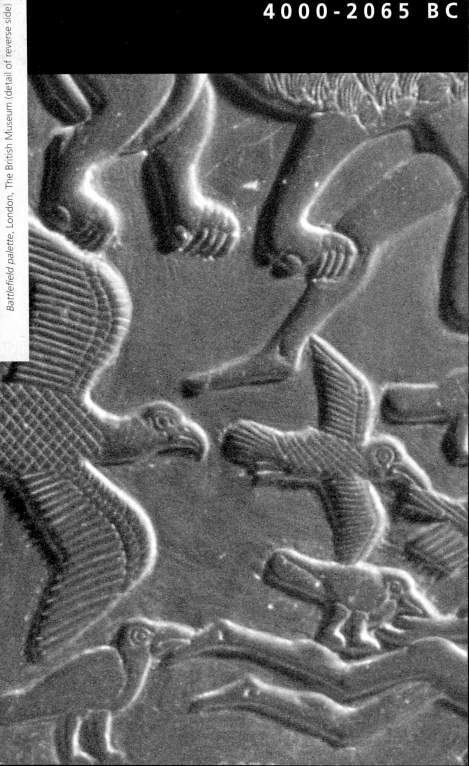

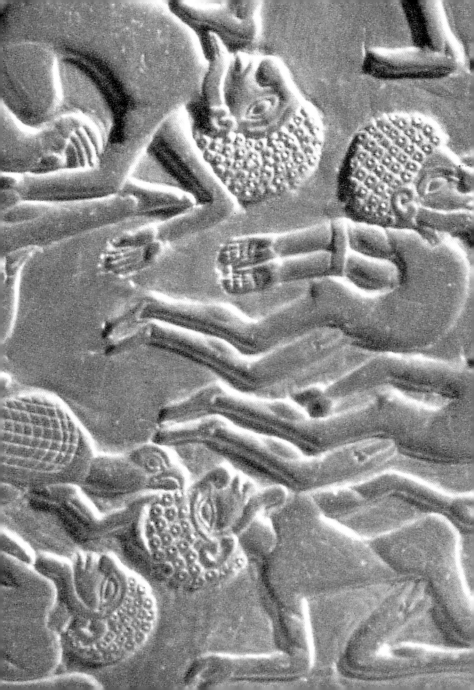

The earliest Egyptian art

One of the first cultural revolutions in human history occurred with the transition from multipurpose implements to specialist objects serving different functions. As well as being more efficient, these were based on forms that existed in nature. Artisans modelled and decorated objects so that they would fit in with their surroundings, in a desire to transpose their own everyday lives into the things they made. As this practice became more widespread, so the individual sensitivities of the artist became more apparent. In Egypt this process lasted hundreds of thousands of years, but gradually accelerated between 20,000 and 4000 BC. During this period, objects acquired characteristics which meant they could immediately be attributed to a single culture, such as that of Naqada I. These heralded the most important feature of Egyptian art throughout its history: the imitation of nature, in accordance with fixed conventions.

▲ *Schist cosmetic palette*, London, The British Museum, EA 36367. During the Naqada I period, Egyptian craftsmen often took their inspiration from nature. This palette was used to grind malachite for cosmetic purposes. A few simple shapes have been added to a circle to create a simplified image of a tortoise.

▲ *Bowl from the Naqada I culture*, Turin, Museo Egizio, S 1827. The shape of the container has been used to suggest a lakeland landscape.

Two aquatic animals appear in the middle, indicating the presence of the lake, and upside-down houses have been placed around the edge. Above these, two hunters are holding some animals on a rope.

▲ *Vases,* London, The British Museum, EA 26636 and 47996. As time passed, Egyptian craftsmen made their work more expressive by placing an increased focus on narrative, seeking new stimuli while remaining true to tradition. The transition to the Naqada II culture was not so much a break with the past as a development of its achievements. There was a significant increase in the production of stone vases, which are believed to have been objects of prestige, and whose shapes were imitated in pottery vessels.

In some cases the makers reproduced the shape of the container in that of the decoration, as in the vase on the left. Pottery vases, on the other hand, tended to use figurative motifs surrounded by repetitive patterns, such as the boat in a Nile landscape on the right-hand vase.

▶ *Knife from Gebel el-Arak,* Paris, Musée du Louvre, E 11517. The figures on the handle have often been cited as showing the influence of Mesopotamia on Egyptian art. The arrangement of the combatants and the boats on the front of the handle possibly suggest this, but the figure of the hero with two lions on the back is a very common theme from contemporary Mesopotamia.

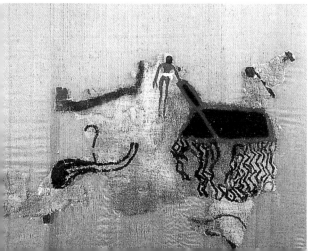

◀ *Painted cloth from Gebelein,* Turin, Museo Egizio, S 17138. The fragmentary nature of this piece makes the decoration difficult to interpret, but it has often been described as depicting a funeral, with stylized male and female figures floating amid houses and boats.

GREAT MASTERPIECES

The battlefield palette

Palettes for eye shadow, such as this large and richly ornamented example from The British Museum, London (EA 20791), were made in the late Predynastic Period. They were placed in temples as offerings to the divinities.

▶ The decoration on the back of the palette is much more static than that on the front. The two herbivores, with very elongated legs and necks, were imaginary creatures. The mirror-image arrangement around the palm tree recalls similar scenes in Mesopotamian art.

◀ The decoration on the front of the battlefield palette is extraordinarily forceful and dynamic. The lion, representing the king, hurls itself on the enemy; it is arranged on two diverging curves, the first arching upwards to symbolize victory and the second trailing downwards. The three vultures in the bottom left-hand corner reproduce the movement of a single bird about to land; the artist has represented the various stages of its flight, and has even shown the arc it describes in the sky by varying its dimensions. The bird is large as it enters the picture, because it is close to the observer, but becomes smaller in the distance and then slightly bigger again when it returns to land.

▼ *Palette of the Libyan tribute*, Cairo, Egyptian Museum, CG 14238. These pictures of animals do not seem to have any narrative purpose, and have been interpreted as depicting a tribute. The boomerang hieroglyph on the top right-hand side of the last register is a reference to Libya.

▲ *Fragment of the bull palette*, Paris, Musée du Louvre, E 11255. The image of the king (here symbolized by a bull) overcoming his enemies occurs frequently on palettes.

The birth of the unitary state

The pharaonic state grew up around 3000 BC as the result of a union between two kingdoms, one in the north and one in the south. This event was crucial for the culture of the whole Nile valley. In art, the existence of a single ruling house led to the development of styles and conventions related to the function of the king who, because he was immortal, rendered them immutable. It was this view that led to the vein of conservatism that runs through all Egyptian art. The three-dimensional art of this period was designed to be viewed only from the front, and was born of a desire to alter the block of stone as little as possible.

Reliefs, made in such a way as to create strong contrasts between light and shade, were used almost exclusively to decorate ceremonial objects offered to the divinities. Although pictures were broadly geometrical in composition, space was not clearly defined. Figures were idealized, and there was often a strong emphasis on musculature, in a pattern that was still far from fully developed.

▲ *Ivory statue of a king,* London, The British Museum, EA 37996. Although its dating has often been questioned, this small sculpture is believed to represent a Early Dynastic king because of the slightly archaic rendering of the facial features.

◀ The *Narmer palette* (Cairo, Egyptian Museum, CG 14176) is one of the first examples to show the figure of the king striking the enemy with a club. This image remained in use in Egypt until the late Roman Period.

The main scene on the palette is arranged along the diagonal axes between the club and the enemy, the falcon (representing the king) and the dignitary, defining the relationships between the various figures.

▼ *Statue of a woman*, Munich, Staatliche Sammlung Ägyptischer Kunst, ÄS 4234. Here, the human figure has been portrayed in a completely flat, frontal view.

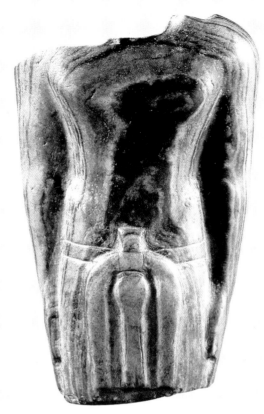

▲ *Fragment of a statuette of a man*, Munich, Staatliche Sammlung Ägyptischer Kunst, ÄS 7149. This sculpture combines an accurately modelled musculature with a geometric rendering of the whole. The striations of the sedimentary rock have been used to emphasize the shape of the body, and give the whole of the statuette a vibrant sense of colour.

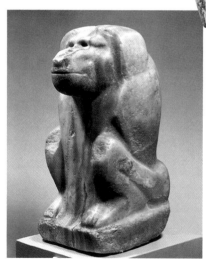

◄ *Statue of a baboon with the name Narmer*, Berlin, Ägyptisches Museum, 22607. The animal's form is reduced to its essentials, the shape of the block of stone almost unchanged.

The 1st and 2nd dynasties

The kings of the first two dynasties came from the region of Abydos, where they had themselves buried in imposing funerary monuments with rectangular superstructures made from unfired mud-brick. This shape has been compared to the masonry bench which appears outside the houses of Egyptian peasants, known in Arabic as a *mastaba*, and the term is now used to refer to this type of tomb.

The period between the 1st and 2nd Dynasties, also known as the Early Dynastic Period, was a formative moment in pharaonic culture. As funerary architecture became increasingly grand and imposing, so art began making more fluid use of space and light and treating surfaces in a more gentle way. The human figure began to extend beyond the bounds of the original block of stone, and three-dimensionality became more important.

▲ *Statue of Khasekhemwy*, Cairo, Egyptian Museum, JE 32161. Although the robe encloses the figure within a fixed composition, its gracefulness heralds that of statues during the subsequent period.

◄ *Stela of King Djet*, Paris, Musée du Louvre, E 11007. The image is entirely dominated by the name of the king (represented by the serpent) written within the *serekh*, a palace with a falcon above it. The most striking feature of the stela is the neat, linear composition, in which the elements are arranged in large empty spaces, giving the stela an enormous force and luminosity. However, the details of the individual figures are slightly crude and heavy.

HISTORIC AND ARTISTIC CONTEXT

▶ A reconstruction of the *mastaba* of Queen Merneith at Abydos. Royal funerary monuments were surrounded by an outer wall, with the tombs of the dead person's servants being placed outside this.

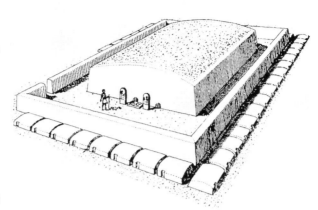

▶ Saqqara, which was the necropolis of Memphis, the first capital of the unified state, contains *mastabas* which are even more impressive than those of the royal necropolis at Abydos. This plan of a tomb dating from the reign of King Djet shows that the outer walls were an alternation of projections and niches, a form with parallels in Mesopotamian architecture.

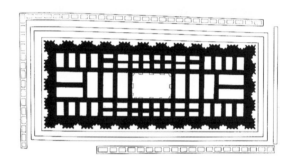

◀ The tomb of Qa'a at Abydos has a funerary chamber entered by a broad staircase and surrounded by magazines used to store goods for the use of the dead person. Nearly all funerary monuments of this kind were built in unfired mud-brick, and stone was used only for the door-frames which sealed the entrances.

The 3rd dynasty: the transition from mud-brick to stone

Egyptian art began to reach full maturity in the early 3rd dynasty, when the introduction of new quarrying and sculpting techniques made stone easier to use. The hardness of this new material meant that unfired brick was completely abandoned in funerary and religious architecture, which was intended to last for all eternity.

Because this was such a sudden change, architects had not yet developed a formal language suitable for structures made entirely of stone, and the first monuments were therefore simply grander versions of buildings which had previously been made from unfired mud-brick and wood. As stone became easier to carve, and sculptors gained the ability to work on a larger scale, so life-size statues became more common. While some figurative sculptures remained true to the shape of the block, others began to place more emphasis on that of the body. Male figures in particular were shown without clothes and in motion, though they were still strictly geometric.

▲ *Wooden panel depicting Hesyra*, Cairo, Egyptian Museum, CG 1427. Hesyra, a functionary, is portrayed in a simple but vibrantly realistic manner.

◄ *Painted limestone statue of Djoser*, Cairo, Egyptian Museum, JE 6008. The figure of the king was found inside the *serdab* (the chamber without an entrance in which the statue of the dead person was placed) close to the king's funerary temple. It had two holes at eye height allowing the king to 'see' the outside world. In ancient Egypt, statues were regarded not as representations of the individual, but as substitutes for them. This image of Djoser is regarded as the earliest life-size stone statue. It retains the austerity and compactness of statues from the previous period, but on a larger scale.

◀ *'The lady of Naples'*, Naples, Museo Archeologico Nazionale, 1076. Long held to be a statue of a woman, this is now believed to depict a male official seated on a throne. The heavy, minimalist modelling reflects the desire to fit the human figure within the block of stone.

◀ *Statues of Sepa and Nesa*, Paris, Musée du Louvre, N 38 and 39. These are among the oldest known examples of lifesize standing sculptures. The figure of Nesa shows features previously noted of female statuary, but that of Sepa derives from two-dimensional art. He is moving forwards, with the staff and sceptre placed in front of his leg and along his arm, in an attempt to show from the front details normally visible only from the side.

▲ *Statue of Princess Redit*, Turin, Museo Egizio, C 3065. The statue contains features of two opposing trends in the earliest Egyptian art. The throne and the lower part of the figure are heavy and compact, acting as a counterpoint to the more graceful upper section, though again the human figure has been circumscribed within geometric forms.

ART AND ARCHITECTURE

The funerary complex of Djoser at Saqqara

The transition from unfired mud-brick to stone created new architectural possibilities, which were immediately exploited to the full in the funerary complex of Djoser at Saqqara. This was built by Imhotep, the king's son (?), who was a brilliant architect.

The central element of the whole structure is the so-called Step Pyramid, which is where the king was buried. This is simply a wider and taller version of the *mastabas* of previous periods, surrounded by a series of buildings which are encircled by a boundary wall. This is decorated with projections and niches, and has fifteen doors, though only the one at the southeast corner actually opens.

The funerary temple is located along the north side of the pyramid, while the southeastern section of the complex is occupied by a series of structures where the rites celebrating the king's jubilee were held. The impression is that of a vast stone stage set, with doors that lead nowhere and buildings which are monumental versions of the wood and mud-brick architecture of earlier times. The southwest corner of the large courtyard which extends to the south of the pyramid contains a building whose top is decorated with a cobra frieze. The underground chambers beneath this building are believed to have housed a statue of the king, whose body was buried at the bottom of the shaft below the Step Pyramid.

▲ The *mastaba* of the original design is still visible at the southeast corner of the Step Pyramid. Larger stones were used when the pyramid was built; smaller ones had originally been used to avoid contrasting too much with the mud bricks employed previously.

◄ The chapels in the jubilee courtyard are stone imitations of the brick and wood structures used to hold the celebrations of the king's rebirth, thus providing an eternal validity to this jubilee ceremony.

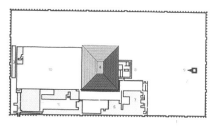

◄ The southeast gate of the funerary complex led into a corridor flanked by engaged, ribbed columns. These are linked by walls to the wall behind them, showing that the construction techniques of the time did not allow self-supporting structures.

▲ Side view of the Step Pyramid and plan of the funerary complex.

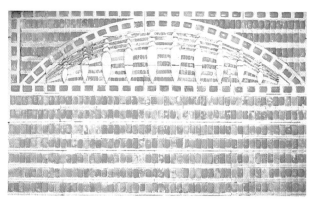

◄ *Panels made from small blue faience tiles,* Cairo, Egyptian Museum, JE 68921. The underground corridors and chambers beneath the funerary complex are decorated with panels similar to the reed mats hanging on the walls of the royal palace, thus preserving them for eternity.

HISTORIC AND ARTISTIC CONTEXT

The beginnings of the Old Kingdom

The belief in the pharaoh's divinity influenced art throughout the early part of the 4th dynasty, during which figures of each king were used as models for all the statuary produced during his reign. This belief is also apparent in the quest for abstraction and austerity in royal sculptures, all of which had an extreme geometry and purity of form which emphasized the pharaoh's difference from and superiority to mere mortals. Although statues of private persons were also based on these ideas, there was a change of direction in that although private persons were seen simply as part of a whole, sculptors also sought to achieve a degree of individuality. Figures in general were highly abstract, but faces were modelled in almost portrait-like detail.

▲ *Quartzite head of a sphinx of Djedefra,* Paris, Musée du Louvre, E 12626. The hollow cheeks and soft, geometric mouth give the king's face a real tension and vibrancy.

◄ *Limestone statues of Rahotep and Nofret,* Cairo, Egyptian Museum, CG 3 and 4. The high seat-backs make the two statues look extremely compact and place the figures within a geometrical framework. The use of different colours emphasizes the different functions served by men and women, and creates oppositions such as indoor/outdoor and movement/immobility.

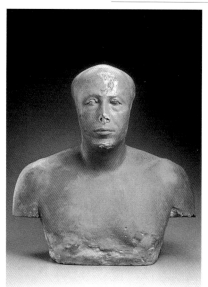

◀ *Diorite statue of Khafra,* Cairo, Egyptian Museum, CG 14716. Each part of the figure fits within a geometric shape, culminating in the trapezoidal form of the headdress. These forms confer a sense of majesty, priestliness and power on the statue.

▲ *Bust of Ankhhaf,* Boston, Museum of Fine Arts, 27442. The irregularly shaped head and clearly defined facial features of this very fine figure make it almost a portrait, though the overall figure is still highly geometrical.

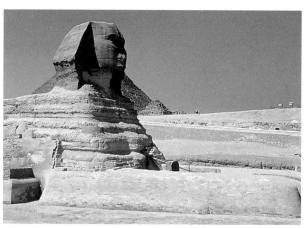

◀ The monumental Sphinx of Giza, cut from a limestone knoll, is a large-scale version of the powerfully austere effigies of Khafra that were more typical of the time. The lion's body with the king's head represents the savage side of royal power.

GREAT MASTERPIECES

Meidum geese

This fragment of wall decoration (Cairo, Egyptian Museum, CG 1742) comes from the *mastaba* of the architect Nefermaat and his wife Atet at Meidum, and is typical of early Old Kingdom art, in which naturalism acts as a counterpoint to abstraction. The scene shows six geese divided into two groups of three; this arrangement is significant because it reflects the way in which the plural was expressed in the ancient Egyptian language.

There are a number of details of movement which prevent the scene from being static. The different sizes of the geese also create a slight sense of perspective, which appears to converge on the centre.

▲ The geese are not like real ones, but are prototypes whose stylized plumage makes them look more like hieroglyphic signs than real animals.

◀ *Fragment of wall decoration with duck-hunting scene,* Copenhagen, Ny Carlsberg Glyptotheck, AEIN 113. A hieroglyphic inscription in the tomb mentions the method probably used to decorate the walls, which involved inlays filled with coloured pastes.

◄ *Fragment of wall decoration depicting hunting and ploughing scenes, from the tomb of Nefermaat and Atet,* Cairo, Egyptian Museum, CG 14. The technique of incising figures on the wall and then filling them with coloured paste was not a success, and was not used anywhere else.

▼ Reconstruction of the northern chapel of Atet showing the probable position of the 'Meidum geese'. Their removal from the wall has taken them out of context; they are not simply a descriptive detail, but part of one of the undisputed masterpieces of Egyptian art.

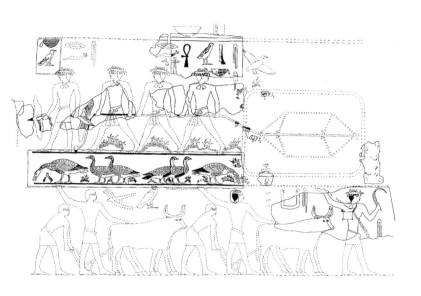

ART AND ARCHITECTURE

The 4th-dynasty pyramids

None of Djoser's immediate successors managed to complete his own funerary monument, and it was not until the reign of Sneferu, the first king of the 4th dynasty, that the pyramid rapidly evolved into its most characteristic form. At least four pyramids are known to date from Sneferu's time, documenting the transition from a stepped structure (as at Meidum) to the tapered outer walls of Dahshur.

The quest for the perfect architectural form culminated in the funerary monument of Khufu, and that of his successors Khafra and Menkaura, at Giza. The pyramid became the symbol of pharaonic civilization, embodying its fundamental characteristics. It was an ordered, geometric monument standing amid the chaos and aridity of the desert, manifesting the existence of the king and his most important function, which was to protect the cosmos from chaos.

The pyramid was an empty symbol, a simple geometric form to which different and sometimes conflicting meanings can be attributed. It has been variously interpreted as a primordial hill, a ramp leading up to the heavens, or a symbol of the rays of the sun. Ultimately, the significance of the pyramids is as difficult to understand as Egyptian society itself, with all its cultural manifestations.

▲ The Step Pyramid at Meidum. Sneferu built this at the beginning of his reign, using the same stepped structure as that of the 3rd dynasty.

▼ The Bent Pyramid at Dahshur. It was designed to be around 150 metres high, but ground subsidence occurred during building, and its angle of inclination was therefore reduced. Then, faced with fine limestone, it was finally abandoned.

▲ The plain of Giza viewed from the south. The funerary complex of Menkaura is visible in the foreground, together with the three small pyramids of the queens. The pyramid of Khafra is in the centre, its summit still partially covered in the original limestone facing. Although less high than the pyramid of Khafra's father Khufu, it looks taller because it is built on a slight rise.

▼ The Great Pyramid of Giza. Khufu succeeded where his father Sneferu had failed, by building his own funerary monument 146.4 metres high. This was classed as one of the seven wonders of the ancient world, and has always aroused the admiration of visitors. Built using stone quarried from the surrounding area, it was originally covered in brilliant white limestone slabs. The chamber containing the king's sarcophagus was built with enormous granite blocks from Aswan. The entrance to the pyramid was on the north side, facing the circumpolar stars, to link the king's eternal presence with that of these stars in the night sky. Because they never set, the Egyptians called them 'the imperishable ones'.

▶ Sections through the pyramids of Sneferu at Dahshur, and those of Khufu, Khafra and Menkaura at Giza.

CHEOPE = KHUFU
MICERINO = MENKAURA
CHEFREN = KHAFRA

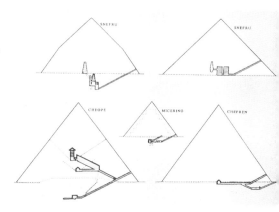

Reserve heads

The name 'reserve heads' was given to this type of sculpture by the German Egyptologist Hermann Junker, who found the first examples in the western necropolis at Giza. Referring to the Pyramid Texts, he believed they were meant as replacements for the head of the dead person in case it was damaged or destroyed. A few dozen reserve heads have been found, most dating from the first half of the 4th dynasty.

◀ *Reserve head,* Boston, Museum of Fine Arts, 14719. The high cheekbones, fleshy lips and nose suggest the subject may have been of African origin. Regardless of their exact function, spare heads show the level of mastery achieved by workshops in the capital, Memphis, and are distinctly naturalistic despite their abstract overall design. The prominent facial features contrast with the simplicity of the head, and the ears are sometimes omitted.

▶ *Reserve head,* Cairo, Egyptian Museum, JE 46216. This shows a member of Khafra's family; although it is one of the most finished, the ears have been left out. The incisions along the hairline have been interpreted as guidelines placed there by the artist. According to more recent theories, reserve heads (which reproduced the individual's features in an abstract way) were models used by artists for statues or reliefs.

▼ *Reserve head,* Vienna, Kunsthistorisches Museum, ÄS 7787. Some reserve heads, such as this one, have very prominent but ambiguous features. This makes it unclear whether they represent men or women.

▼ *Reserve head,* Berkeley, Phoebe Hearst Museum of Anthropology, 6-19767. This is believed to be an effigy of Kanefer, in whose tomb it was found. It is one of the most finished of all. The eyebrows and hairline are shown; the ears have been chiselled away.

▼ *Reserve head,* Boston, Museum of Fine Arts, 21328. Here the facial features are surprisingly delicate, and have been reduced to their essentials. The hairline is absent, and the eyebrows have been barely outlined.

The transition from the 4th to the 5th dynasty

The period of transition between the 4th and 5th dynasties saw a series of cultural changes which had major repercussions for Egyptian society. Most important of all was the increased emphasis on sun worship, which also resulted in a new role for the king; instead of being a god with absolute powers, he became the son of Ra, the sun. In art, there was greater freedom of expression and sense of movement. The static, hieratic nature of early 4th-dynasty statuary began to break down during the reign of Menkaura, and sculptures acquired an irrepressible force as though trying to free themselves from the stone from which they were fashioned. This style gathered pace during the reigns of successive kings; statues acquired a much greater feeling of liberty and movement, and an unparalleled grace and lightness.

▼ *Graywacke triad of Menkaura*, Cairo, Egyptian Museum, JE 46499. The king is portrayed between the goddess Hathor and a personification of the 7th *nome* (district) of Upper Egypt.

▼ *Graywacke statue of King Menkaura and Queen Khamerernebty*, Boston, Museum of Fine Arts, 11.1738. In this extraordinary masterpiece, the king's facial features have been used also as a model for those of the queen.

◀ *Gneiss statue of Sahura and a divinity*, New York, The Metropolitan Museum of Art, 18.2.4. The fact that the king is shown seated on a throne with the divinity walking beside him, and the two figures' different proportions, reflect the artistic changes of the 5th dynasty. Forms acquired a greater sense of movement, and compositions were less geometric and frontal than during the previous period.

▼ *Wooden statue of Kaaper, known as 'Sheikh el-Balad'*, Cairo, Egyptian Museum, CG 34. In this sculpture the artist has been freed from the limitations imposed by the use of a stone block, with vividly realistic results.

◀ *Painted limestone sculpture of seated scribe*, Cairo, Egyptian Museum, CG 36. The empty space between the arms and chest, the raised edges of the wig and the use of brilliant colour all give this statue a great delicacy despite its use of strongly geometric forms.

The end of the Old Kingdom

During the 5th and 6th dynasties, the ruling class acquired increasing importance within the pharaonic state. Wealthy officials had themselves buried in large tombs with stone superstructures imitating the royal *mastabas* of the Early Dynastic period. The interior walls were designed to resemble the rooms of a house, richly decorated with reliefs painted in brilliant colours showing aspects of everyday life, including trivial and sometimes whimsically amusing details. Increasing numbers of ordinary people had themselves portrayed alone or with their families in miniature masterpieces which combined close observation of the individual with increasingly innovative modelling.

◄ *Limestone statue of the dwarf Seneb and his family*, Cairo, Egyptian Museum, JE 51280.

▼ *Limestone statue of Kaemked*, a priest. Cairo, Egyptian Museum, CG 119.

HISTORIC AND ARTISTIC CONTEXT

◀ *Relief showing a river being forded, from the tomb of Ty at Saqqara.* Despite naturalistic details such as the transparent water, the cow raising its head towards the calf and the rendering of light and movement, this piece still bears the traces of strictly formal artistic canons.

▼ *Limestone group depicting a man and his family,* New York, Brooklyn Museum of Art, 3717E. The artist has used differing proportions and staggered planes to create an original family group with a strong feeling of movement.

▶ *Relief depicting a hippopotamus hunt,* Berlin, Ägyptisches Museum, 2/70. In scenes like this, a carefully ordered composition of geometric elements can be used to create decorative effects quite apart from the reality it depicts.

▼ *Relief depicting navigation in a papyrus skiff,* Berlin, Ägyptisches Museum, 15420. The arrangement of the lotus flowers around the boat shows a desire to represent reality in an accurate manner.

Statuette of Meryra-ankhnes and Pepy II

The alabaster statuette of Queen Meryra-ankhnes and Pepy II (New York, Brooklyn Museum of Art, 39119) is a remarkable example of late Old-Kingdom art. However, the most surprising innovation is the fact that the mother and son are depicted from two different points of view.

▶ The queen is probably designed to be viewed mainly from the front. The space between the arms and chest and graceful, delicate limbs are typical of the late Old Kingdom.

◄ *Alabaster statuette of Pepy I,* New York, Brooklyn Museum of Art, 39.120. Although completely frontal, this small statue anticipates that of Pepy II with his mother (on page 36). The falcon on the back of the seat allows the piece to be viewed in two ways. It can be rotated through 90 degrees, or turned right round, making the back into a stela with the king's name inscribed in the *serekh,* his palace-shaped symbol.

◄ The frontal view of the king (who is probably a boy, although shown as a small-scale adult) is of secondary significance to that of the queen. His importance is marked by his position in the centre of the composition. The block beneath his feet stresses the variety of volumes in this sculpture.

► *Alabaster statuette of Pepy II,* Cairo, Egyptian Museum, JE 50616. Despite being only 16 cm high, this piece has many of the characteristics of the art of its time. The slightly spread legs and the space beneath the arms give it a sense of lightness and movement, but the composition as a whole is still geometrical.

The First Intermediate Period

▲ *Scene from the tomb of Ankhtyfy at Moalla.* In two-dimensional art, the picture was divided up in an attempt to create perspective. In this scene, the space between the two figures is filled by objects which in real life would be hidden from the observer by the hearth.

During the 6th dynasty, Egypt underwent a profound crisis which led to the disintegration of the unitary state. The *nomes* (districts) became autonomous, and were ruled by local governors who created dynasties of their own. The advent of these 'new men', as they were called, gave rise to the development of a new world view in which the individual acquired increasing importance within society.

In art, this was reflected in a provincial style which was less rigid than that of the capital and showed an increased interest in colour and movement. Wall painting replaced painted reliefs almost everywhere, and the ordered and carefully-proportioned positioning of figures in space was deliberately abandoned.

▼ *Wall decoration from the tomb of Iti at Gebelein,* Turin, Museo Egizio, S 14354. Here, oblique lines have been used to break up the division of the scene into registers. These create different spaces and surfaces; for example the desert is recognizable from the gazelles grazing in it, and the steps lead the procession of porters upwards.

▼ Scenes in the tomb of Iti exploit colour contrasts; little importance is given to the proportions of the figures.

◀ The tombs of provincial governors (in this case, that of Uahka II at Qau el-Kebir) were often excavated from rocky hillsides recalling the shape of pyramids.

◀ *Wooden model from the tomb of Mesehti at Asyut,* Cairo, Egyptian Museum, CG 258. The differences in the soldiers' heights, clothing and skin colour reflect the artist's desire to depict reality as accurately as possible.

▼ *Butchery scene from the tomb of Iti.* The contrast between the red blood and the white animal confers a harshness on the scene.

Wooden models from the tomb of Niankhpepy

Models of men and women engaged in a variety of activities began to replace wall reliefs in the tombs of private individuals from the late Old Kingdom onwards. These painted wooden ones from the rock tomb of Niankhpepy at Meir are typical of the art of the First Intermediate Period.

▶ The *Three porters* (Cairo, Egyptian Museum, CG 250) creates the impression of forward movement by showing the figures growing larger as they approach us, so attempting to reproduce the rhythm of walking.

▶ *Statuette of a farm worker*, Cairo, Egyptian Museum, CG 249.

◀ This *Small model* (Cairo, Egyptian Museum, CG 244) depicts the preparation of dough for baking and brewing. Bread and beer were the staples of the Egyptian diet.

▲ *Statuette of a porter,* Cairo, Egyptian Museum, CG 241. The perfect proportions of this work show the influence of the Old Kingdom.

The end of the First Intermediate Period

W ith the passing of time, the provincial states consolidated their positions and began to encroach on their neighbours. Egypt was very soon racked by internecine warfare and social unrest, and the absence of a central body to regulate the effects of annual flooding of the Nile led to frequent shortages throughout the country.

The city of Thebes (now Luxor) benefited from this situation by rapidly consolidating its own power at the expense of its immediate neighbours. The 11th-dynasty kings of Thebes conquered the north, and in a matter of years had placed the whole of the Nile valley under a single crown.

There is evidence that one or more artistic schools existed in Upper Egypt during the Old Kingdom. Some of their creations have survived and, although they imitate the modelling and styles of Theban art, they differ from it in their treatment of volumes and absence of balanced proportions. This tradition influenced Theban art during the latter part of the First Intermediate Period, but its forms and styles took their inspiration from the older northern traditions, though with a greater force and freedom of composition.

▲ *Small wooden model,* Cairo, Egyptian Museum, JE 46724. This cattle census is one of a series of small, complex models depicting aspects of everyday life that were found in the tomb of Meketra.

◀ *Small painted wooden model of a cowshed,* Munich, Staatliche Sammlung Ägyptischer Kunst. The tradition of placing models in tombs lasted throughout the First Intermediate Period, and the models became increasingly elaborate.

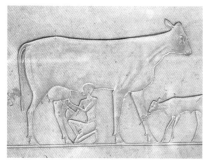

▲ *Limestone statue of General Antef,* Cairo, Egyptian Museum, JE 89858 + 91169. This is a good example of the Upper Egyptian school of sculpture.

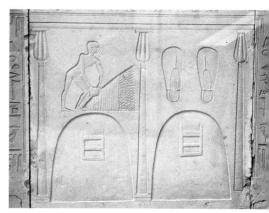

▲ *Sarcophagus of Princess Kawit,* Cairo, Egyptian Museum, JE 47397. These panels show scenes from everyday life, with charming details such as the cow apparently shedding a tear as it is milked, and the mannered gestures of the princess drinking and the maidservant attending to her hair.

The stiff composition recalls the more classical style of the Old Kingdom.

▶ *Sarcophagus of Ashayt,* Cairo, Egyptian Museum, JE 47267. Space is used here without the restriction of register lines.

The temple of Mentuhotep II at Deir el-Bahri

ART AND ARCHITECTURE

The Old-Kingdom pyramids were the centrepieces of larger temple complexes in which the king was worshipped. During the First Intermediate Period, these temples were excavated from hillsides, replacing pyramids but more or less exactly recalling their shape. It was this process of change which led Mentuhotep II to build his funerary temple at Deir el-Bahri, on the west bank of the Nile opposite Luxor. This had a vast natural amphitheatre with a pyramid-shaped peak above it, and below Mentuhotep's architects designed a terraced temple preceded by a courtyard, which was planted with numerous rows of sycomores and tamarisks.

On the first terrace there was a huge pillared hall surrounded by a portico. At its centre was a massive masonry structure whose exact function is unknown; according to the most recent hypothesis, it was the base of a structure recalling the primeval hill from which the world emerged.

Beyond this, a porticoed courtyard led in to a pillared hall at the end of which, buried in the mountain, was a sanctuary dedicated to Amun and the deified king. The tomb itself, a granite-clad chamber, was excavated more than 150 metres inside the mountain.

▶ *Statue of Mentuhotep II,* Cairo, Egyptian Museum, JE 36195. This was found in a chamber at the end of a long corridor dug beneath the courtyard in front of the temple at Deir el-Bahri. The heavy forms and brilliantly contrasting colours are typical of the more classical tradition of Upper Egyptian sculpture.

▼ Ruins of the temple of Mentuhotep II at Deir el-Bahri. At the centre are the foundations of a masonry structure on which a replica of the primeval hill is believed to have been built.

▼ Plan of the temple of Mentuhotep II at Deir el-Bahri. The structure is designed as a series of three almost square modules, each an architectural unit in its own right, designed to fit in perfectly with the rocky landscape behind it.

▲ *Mentuhotep II wearing the red crown, in a relief from Deir el-Bahri.* London, The British Museum, EA 1397. The modelling is inspired by Old Kingdom art, the rigidity of which is offset by a lively spirit typical of local schools of sculpture.

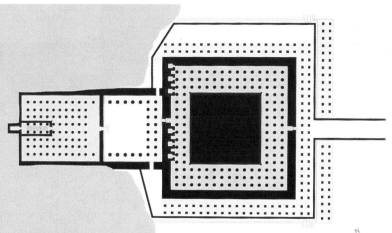

The beginnings of the Middle Kingdom

The 12th dynasty was founded by a vizier named Amenemhat. He and his immediate successors had the difficult task of consolidating the recently reunified state, renewing the credibility of royalty and cleaning up the central administrative apparatus.

One of the first changes made by the new dynasty was to move the centre of government to the north. A new capital was established near el-Lisht, a few dozen kilometres from Memphis, the site of the capital throughout the Old Kingdom. The explicit references to this period, reflecting a desire to resume the style interrupted during the First Intermediate Period, had repercussions for the whole of the official culture of the time. Royal reliefs and sculptures showed a clear return to styles and proportions inspired by courtly purity, dominated by geometry and harmony of form and the ordered arrangement of figures. Once again, funerary complexes were centred on pyramids, this time consisting of unfired mud-brick structures (though that of Amenemhat I is made of stone), with only the inner chambers and facing being made from limestone.

However, Egyptian provincial art continued to develop a language of its own. There are some magnificent examples in the tomb paintings of Middle and Upper Egypt, which depicted natural phenomena in an increasingly realistic way.

▲ *Reliefs from the White Chapel of Senusret I.* The reliefs at Karnak are energetically modelled and divided up in an orderly manner, with every space being filled with figures or hieroglyphics.

◄ The architecture and provincial-style painting in the tombs of the nobles at Beni Hassan, such as that of Khety (BH 17), are masterpieces of unsurpassed beauty dating from the beginning of the 12th dynasty.

▶ The White Chapel of Senusret I was used as a way station for the god's boat when it was carried along in procession. The chapel was dismantled and reused as filling material. It was recovered from within one of the pylons of the temple of Amun-Ra, and reconstructed in its entirety.

◀ Statue of a king with a white crown, Cairo, Egyptian Museum, JE 44951. The king depicted may be Senusret I or II. The harmonious proportions of the king's shapely body and the regularity of the facial features recall the typical characteristics of Egyptian art during the Old Kingdom.

▼ Ten limestone statues of Senusret I, Cairo, Egyptian Museum, CG 411-420; made as a series for the royal funerary temple at el-Lisht.

Female statuary of the Middle Kingdom

Throughout pharaonic history, the female figure was shown in art with eternal, immutable youth and idealized beauty. It had a sensuality which was sometimes merely hinted at, and at other times was very prominent. And it always had connotations of fertility, from the very oldest prehistoric figurines with strongly emphasized female attributes through to the fully formed statues of Ptolemaic queens.

Artists used the female figure to convey the ideal of eternity upon which the whole of Egyptian culture was premised, and the promise of perpetual reincarnation created by the possibility of future maternity.

Although every period produced female images of extraordinary beauty, those of the Middle Kingdom were without equal. The influence of courtly canons, in which the human figure was placed within a precise geometric framework, blended with the increased realism of the First Intermediate Period. This attractive combination of abstraction and naturalism resulted in elegantly proportioned female figures which emphasized the idea of fertility without detracting from that of female beauty.

◀ *Statue of a woman breastfeeding a baby boy*, Berlin, Ägyptisches Museum, 14078. This theme had been used since the late Old Kingdom, but was taken up with a greater attention to naturalistic detail. A series of curves have been used to convey the intimate relationship which unites the two figures.

▲ *Ivory statuette of a woman*, Paris, Musée du Louvre, E 14697. Despite the loss of the head and arms, the curved vertical lines of the robe and the woman's body make this an abstract but sensual creation.

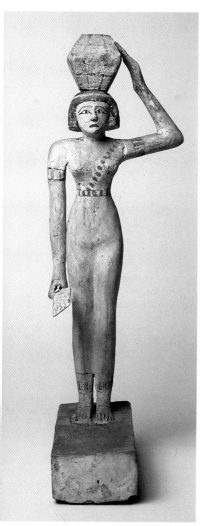

◀ *Wooden statue of a servant girl,* Turin, Museo Egizio, 23986. The rigid figure and slender limbs are typical of provincial art of the period.

▼ *'Concubine' for the dead,* Cairo, Egyptian Museum, JE 44710. It promoted fertility in women and virility in men.

◀ *Wooden head of a woman,* Cairo, Egyptian Museum, JE 39390. A heavy wig frames an extremely lively and attractive face, giving this little sculpture a transcendent beauty.

The end of the Middle Kingdom

Despite the large amount of building carried out by nearly all the kings of the Middle Kingdom, very little remains of their work today. The only vestiges of their pyramids are imposing piles of unfired mud-bricks still visible in the area between Dahshur and El Fayum. Religious buildings were often dismantled, reused and rebuilt from new during the Ptolemaic Period. The only ones to have survived are the little temples at Qasr el-Sagha and Medinet Madi; the latter is the only one to have retained its decoration, consisting of simple, elegant reliefs, from the time of Amenemhat III and Amenemhat IV.

However, numerous examples of royal statuary have survived from this period. Their development can be precisely traced from the regular facial features of Senusret I to the increasingly prominent and dramatic features of later kings. Ordinary persons continued to have themselves portrayed using the canons of royal statuary, probably as a way of demonstrating their loyalty to the crown. The types of statues became increasingly diversified, with a strong preference for courtly models. The body is often enclosed in clothing which turns the sculpture into a succession of geometric surfaces. The 13th dynasty continued along this route, but the statues of this period lacked some of the energy of the previous period despite their considerable artistry.

▶ *Granite statue of Senusret III,* Cairo, Egyptian Museum, RT 18.4.22.4. The large ears are typical of royal statuary of the Middle Kingdom.

▶ *Statue of Khertihotep,* Berlin, Ägyptisches Museum, 15700. The pose is very ancient, though the features echo those of contemporary royal statues and the wig with obliquely cut lower edges is typical of the period.

◀ *Sphinx of Senusret III,* New York, The Metropolitan Museum of Art, 17.9.2. The heavy eyelids and sunken features convey inner strength, and also the weight of responsibility derived from governance.

◀ *Painted limestone statue of Hotep*, Cairo, Egyptian Museum, JE 48857. This unusual statue portrays an individual seated on a chair with high arms. It is sometimes related to the block statue, which suited the Egyptian taste for human figures enclosed within a rigid geometric framework.

▲ *13th-dynasty head of a king*, Cairo, Egyptian Museum, JE 54857.

▼ *Statue of Wahibre-Hor (13th dynasty)*, Cairo, Egyptian Museum, CG 259.

Portraits of Amenemhat III

R̲oyal portraits reached their height during the reign of Amenemhat III, whose features are depicted with a combination of powerful tension and great severity.

▲ *Sphinx of Amenemhat III from Tanis,* Cairo, Egyptian Museum, CG 394. Here, greater than usual emphasis has been placed on the sphinx's power and ferocity. The king's face seems almost to emerge from the lion's body, rather than being imposed upon it, and the impression of majesty is increased by the unusually large base, which draws the eye towards the lower part of the sculpture. The image is that of a king of incomparable power, and the face has a luminous austerity.

◄ Statue of Amenemhat III from Mit Fares, Cairo, Egyptian Museum, CG 395. The head of a leopard on the left shoulder indicates that the king is also a priest. The heavy wig is a rare feature, and probably refers to a connection with the primeval gods.

◄ Statue of Amenemhat III from Hawara, Cairo, Egyptian Museum, CG 385. Portraits of this king vary a great deal; in this one, the facial features are almost boyish.

▲ Statue of Amenemhat III walking, Cairo, Egyptian Museum, CG 42015. The fully frontal view is characteristic of statuary of the Middle Kingdom.

The Second Intermediate Period

HISTORIC AND ARTISTIC CONTEXT

The weakness of the kings who reigned from the late Middle Kingdom onwards led to a new fragmentation within Egypt. This was exploited by peoples of Near Eastern origin (commonly known as the Hyksos) who had settled in the Nile Delta some time previously, to create an independent state. From here, they exercised a degree of control over the whole of the rest of Middle Egypt.

The country was reunified by Thebes during the 17th dynasty, after a long struggle in which the Hyksos were defeated. The art of this period reverted to a provincial style, but lacked the vigour of the First Intermediate Period.

The real innovation is apparent from current finds at the excavations of Tell el-Dabaa, where the Hyksos had their capital. The architectural remains and vestiges of wall decorations show the presence of a cosmopolitan, Mediterranean society in which Aegean and Egyptian art existed side by side with Syro-Palestinian architecture.

▶ *Fragment of plaster* and *Reconstruction of a young acrobat beside a palm tree,* Cairo, Egyptian Museum, TD-8425 [179]. The ruins believed to be those of the royal palace of the Hyksos in Tell el-Dabaa have provided many fragments of dancing and bull-leaping scenes. The clothing, figures and style of painting all show without doubt that this form of decoration was Minoan in origin. These recent finds, together with religious buildings identical to Syro-Palestinian ones and pure Egyptian-style statues bearing the names of Hyksos kings, show that this was the first truly pan-Mediterranean culture.

▲ *Painted limestone stela of Mentuhotep,* Berlin, Ägyptisches Museum, 22708. Artists in both the First and Second Intermediate Periods tended to use bright colours to offset the lack of order in their overall compositions. Unlike the earlier period, the art of the later period did not reflect the cultural development of Egyptian society and therefore lacked any motivation of its own. Its products were attempts to imitate the works of the past, but it did not have the formal means to do this.

▼ *Bull-leaping scene,* Heraklion, Archaeological Museum (from the east wing of the palace of Knossos), and *Young man jumping over the head of a bull,* Cairo, Egyptian Museum, TD-7998 [150]. The similarities between this scene and that on the painted plaster from the palace of Tell el-Dabaa show the close connections between the Hyksos state and Crete. Contacts between Egypt and the Aegean islands are known to have existed at the beginning of the 12th dynasty because of the many Minoan vases and fragments of ceramics found at various sites in the Nile valley.

This two-way relationship was probably based mainly on trade; a number of Egyptian objects bearing the cartouches of Hyksos kings have been found in Crete.

▶ *Statuette of Princess Ahhotep,* Paris, Musée du Louvre, AE 2958. Few works of art survive from the period from the 13th to the 17th dynasties. This statuette dates from the 17th, and shows no major stylistic changes from female figures from the Middle Kingdom. However, it is much more rigid, and does not have the intense vitality and sensuality of earlier works.

57

The early New Kingdom

As in the Middle Kingdom, the reunification of the country had a major influence on the culture of the early 18th dynasty. The kings regarded themselves as the heirs of the purest pharaonic tradition, and created works of art and architecture whose abstract, idealized forms recalled those of the Old Kingdom.

A substantial change occurred with the advent of Hatshepsut, the wife of Thutmose II, who proclaimed herself pharaoh and had herself portrayed as a man and with the attributes of a king. The need to adapt female features to a male body, combined with the archaicizing taste of the period, created a style in which formal perfection took precedence over physical realism.

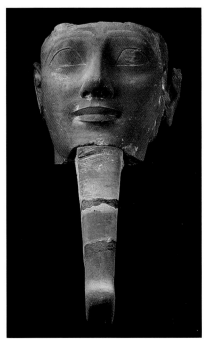

◀ *Colossal painted limestone head of Thutmose I,* Cairo, Egyptian Museum, JE 38235. The return to forms and proportions inspired by the Old Kingdom brought an end to the tradition of portraiture found in 12th-dynasty art. The very large eyes and smiling mouth show the persistence of trends from Theban provincial statuary.

▼ Alabaster way station of Amenhotep I at Karnak. The simple lines of this small building typify the style of the early New Kingdom.

▲ *Torso of Queen Hatshepsut*, Leiden, Rijksmuseum van Oudheden, 10054 (the head is a cast of an original which is in New York). During the first few years of her reign, Hatshepsut had herself portrayed as a woman, but with the attributes of a king, such as the *nemes,* or headcloth, and the uraeus or cobra symbol on the forehead.

▲ *Colossal head of Hatshepsut from Deir el-Bahri,* Cairo, Egyptian Museum, JE 56259 + 56262. This is another example of how Hatshepsut portrayed herself in the likeness of a man, with feminine features but with a pharaoh's typical attributes and clothing. Here, the desire for formal perfection took precedence over accurate portrayal.

▶ *Senenmut and Neferura,* Cairo, Egyptian Museum, CG 42114. Senenmut, a senior official, has used the block statue form to emphasize his role as tutor to Princess Neferura, whose head appears to emerge from the stone.

ART AND ARCHITECTURE

The temple of Hatshepsut at Deir el-Bahri

Hatshepsut decided to have her own temple built at Deir el-Bahri, just to the north of Mentuhotep II's. She used the same terrace structure but on a larger scale, and integrated it more with the cliff behind it.

This imposing architectural complex served various practical and ideological purposes, one of which was to ensure that the queen was worshipped and emphasize her right to the throne by affirming her relationship with Amun-Ra.

The temple also served as the arrival point for the 'beautiful festival of the valley', the area's most important annual religious celebration. A statue of the god was transported there by boat and placed in a sanctuary dug into the mountain at the back of the third terrace. The temple was decorated with magnificent reliefs which recounted Hatshepsut's supposed divine birth and the most important events of her reign. Considerable space was devoted to the journey to the fabled land of Punt by the queen's soldiers, who went there in search of incense trees to dedicate to Amun-Ra.

The temple of Hatshepsut was built in fifteen years, during which it was redesigned several times. A significant number of statues of the queen, including two of colossal size and around a hundred and twenty sphinxes, completed the rich decoration of the complex.

▲ *The queen of Punt,* Cairo, Egyptian Museum, JE 14276, is shown as an extremely fat woman in an image combining close observation of reality with a strong vein of caricature.

▼ The temple of Hatshepsut at Deir el-Bahri, seen from the north.

▼ One of the changes made during the course of the work was the addition of a small chapel dedicated to the goddess Hathor, built into the rocks south of the temple's middle terrace. This was preceded by a small hall of columns with capitals in the form of the head of Hathor.

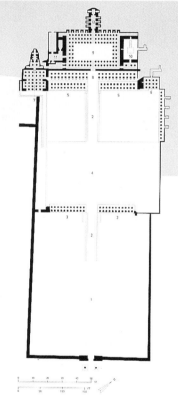

▲ Plan of the temple of Hatshepsut.

▶ Detail of a relief from the chapel of Hathor, showing soldiers at a festival.

Thutmose III and his immediate successors

Before proclaiming herself pharaoh, Hatshepsut had acted as regent for the young Thutmose III, the son of Thutmose II and Queen Aset. When Hatshepsut died after reigning for twenty-three years, Thutmose III finally ascended the throne that was his by right. He turned bitterly against the memory of the stepmother who for so long had relegated him to a secondary role, but did not destroy her temple. Instead he adapted it to his own ends by chiselling away the images of Hatshepsut and replacing her name with those of himself and his father.

Thutmose then decided to abandon this project and had a temple built to himself, again at Deir el-Bahri but in a higher location, between those of his predecessors.

Thutmose III's reign was a time of strong expansion into the Near East and Nubia, and it was during this period that Egyptian rule reached its greatest extent. His son Amenhotep II and nephew Thutmose IV both followed similar policies during their reigns, and also consolidated the power of the pharaonic state by marrying foreign princesses.

The art of this period followed the route begun by Hatshepsut, and was characterized by its simple, brilliant treatment of surfaces. The style of royal faces followed the form established for Hatshepsut, but in a more masculine way. The emphasis remained on ordered, geometric lines that conveyed a sense of abstract eternity.

▼ The *Decoration of the tomb of Thutmose III in the Valley of the Kings* is designed to resemble an enormous papyrus unrolled on the walls and containing funerary texts. It is dominated by red and black, with stylized hieroglyphs and figures. The oval shape of the funerary chamber itself reproduces the form of the cartouche with the king's name inscribed inside.

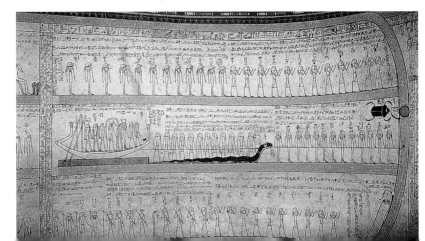

▲ *Green schist statue of Thutmose III*, Luxor, Museum of Egyptian Art, J 2. The very graceful face of this statue has been built up using a series of curves which contrast with the precise geometry of the headdress. The body is greatly simplified, with the various masses being composed in an abstract and luminous way.

▲ *Graywacke statue of Amenhotep II standing*, Cairo, Egyptian Museum, CG 42077. The undecorated headdress emphasizes the softness of the composition, with its youthful-looking body.

◀ *Block from the third pylon of Karnak*, Luxor, Museum of Egyptian Art, J 129. It highlights the sporting prowess of Amenhotep II: in a chariot, he shoots arrows at a target.

The temple of Amun-Ra at Karnak

ART AND ARCHITECTURE

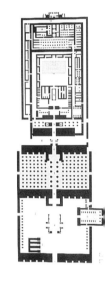

At the end of the First Intermediate Period, the Theban god Amun-Ra became increasingly important, sharing the fortunes of the royal house. The oldest remains of the temple at Karnak dedicated to him date from the 12th dynasty. Fragments of buildings from this period have been found dismantled and reused as filling material in structures erected by Egyptian kings down to the Ptolemaic Period.

From the New Kingdom onwards, every great pharaoh added to the temple complex at Karnak. The central body of it was built around the courtyard dating from the Middle Kingdom, and the structures which surround it today (most famous of which is the 'Festival Hall') mainly date from the reign of Thutmose III. His successors enlarged the building along two different axes, a main one towards the west and a secondary one leading southwards, where the temple of Amun-Ra's consort, Mut, was located.

The biggest expansions were carried out by the Ramesside and 25th-dynasty kings and the Ptolemies. A processional avenue flanked by sphinxes, now believed to date from the 30th dynasty, connected the temple of Karnak with that of Luxor four kilometres to the south.

▲ Plan of the main body of the temple of Amun-Ra at Karnak.

▼ The entrance is flanked by an avenue of sphinxes with rams' heads dating from the Ramesside period. The identification of Amun-Ra as a ram occurred during the New Kingdom.

▲▼ A hypostyle hall of 134 huge columns grew up around the axial colonnade built by Amenhotep III, Sety I and Rameses II. The tall central columns have capitals in the shape of open papyri, while those around the sides take the form of closed papyri. The impression is of being in an immense thicket of petrified papyrus.

▼ The obelisk of Queen Hatshepsut is more than 30 metres high, and is the sole survivor of a pair placed by her in the hypostyle hall of Thutmose I. Texts state that the top was covered in electrum, an alloy of gold and silver, to reflect the rays of the sun god Ra, to whom it was also dedicated. Small monolithic obelisks are known to have existed as early as the 6th dynasty.

1550-1075 BC

Theban painting in the first half of the 18th dynasty

From the 18th dynasty onwards, senior government officials living in Thebes had themselves buried in rock tombs whose interiors were decorated with magnificent paintings. These depicted scenes from everyday life with the emphasis on activities in which the dead person was directly involved, funeral scenes, and in nearly all cases scenes from the underworld. The latter two themes were treated in accordance with religious and other traditional conventions, but the scenes from everyday life showed a much greater freedom based on close and sometimes entertaining observation of real life.

Although the paintings were rigidly divided into registers, the surface treatment showed an inventiveness unequalled in Egyptian art. One example is the tomb of Sennefer, where the irregularities in the ceiling have been exploited to give added realism to the everyday scenes on the walls of the tomb. Artists also used the limited means at their disposal to create movement and perspective through foreshortening, for example in the group of musicians and dancers in the tomb of Nebamun. The vitality of these paintings sometimes extends to more traditional scenes; one example is the banquet scene in the tomb of Rekhmira, where the graceful twisting of the figure of a girl acts as the focal point of the whole painting.

▲ *Two figures of young men with arrows from the tomb of Qenamun* (TT 93). These show a clear symmetry in their arrangement of lines and choice of colours.

▼ *Funeral banquet scene from the tomb of Rekhmira* (TT 100), detail.

◀ *Ceiling of the tomb of Sennefer* (TT 99). The ceiling decoration is a vividly naturalistic imitation of a pergola covered with vine tendrils, highlighting the ordinariness of the scenes depicted on the walls.

▼ *Workers in the fields from the tomb of Menna* (TT 69). This theme often occurs in Theban tomb decoration. The peasants labouring in the barley fields are surrounded by a throng of figures engaged in other activities, in a scene full of life and movement.

▲ ▼ *Group of musicians and dancers* and *Hunting in the marshes* from the tomb of Nebamun (TT 146?), London, The British Museum, EA 37984 and 37977. The first seems to show a kind of primitive perspective, while the second employs brilliant colours.

The decoration of the tomb of Nakht

ART AND ARCHITECTURE

The tomb of Nakht (TT 52) dates from the reign of Thutmose IV, when Theban painting had reached maturity and consolidated a repertoire of traditional scenes. However, the style of the figures is fresh and delicate, and the varied use of space and episodes from everyday life are highly inventive. The whole scheme of decoration shows the fertile period which Theban art had entered, and its seemingly inexhaustible creativity.

As in other tombs, the canonical scenes in the tomb of Nakht (such as the figure of the dead man and his wife) are more formal and static, whereas those depicting everyday life are much more freely portrayed.

The artists who painted the decoration show a strong interest in movement and perspective, and have sought to use the available forms of representation to expand their art in time and space. Some of the figures are such humorous caricatures that it is easy to forget they are part of the decoration of a tomb. The artists have shown the more entertaining side of life, perhaps trying to forget that death is never far away.

◀ *Barley cultivation.* This sequence reads from the bottom upwards. The wavy line at the bottom indicates that the peasants are hoeing an area of land on the edge of the desert, which is uncultivated and therefore chaotic. In the register above this, the artist has shown an amusing episode in which a

peasant jumps into the air to press down the basket full of barley. The bowed figure below him is smaller, indicating that he is further away.

The winnowing scene at the top places a great deal of emphasis on the movement of the men's forearms.

▲ *Banqueting scene.* This scene includes the portrayal of the blind harpist which has made the tomb of Nakht famous. The two groups of women seated behind him are linked by the crossed arms of the woman in the centre. The scene at the bottom is constructed around the three musicians.

▲ *The three musicians of Nakht* are one of the masterpieces of New-Kingdom Egyptian painting. They are arranged in a rhythmical order which echoes the musicality of the scene. Attention is focused on the central figure, whose nudity and movement contrasts with those on either side of her.

◄ *Hunting in the marshes.* This scene appears in a number of Egyptian tombs from the Old Kingdom, where the papyrus always serves merely as a decorative background. During the 18th dynasty, even greater emphasis was placed on this decorative role. The figure of the deceased tomb-owner in the boat is repeated twice, once fowling and once fishing. It confers a degree of symmetry on the scene, though this is continually interrupted by variations in the whole series of details. The scene below this one depicts viticulture. The peasant crouching in the centre of the lower register is shown splitting open ducks for drying and preserving.

The 18th dynasty: Amenhotep III

The reign of Amenhotep III was a time of peace in Egypt. Queen Tiy, who had a great deal of influence at the court, was the daughter of an official from Akhmim and thus, almost uniquely for her time, not of royal origin.

The art of this period showed an increasing interest in line and form which was particularly apparent in facial features; these were either shown as abstract geometric entities, or exaggerated, or highlighted using unnatural-looking lines. The rendering of male faces was particularly interesting, because two different techniques were used to deprive them of their masculinity. In some cases the features were softened and feminized, and in others the proportions were distinctly girlish.

Towards the end of his reign, Amenhotep III had himself portrayed with an obese body. This was the first time this had been done by a king, and anticipated the art of the period which followed.

▲ *Amenhotep III and the god Sobek,* Luxor, Museum of Egyptian Art, J 155. This statue combines beauty of form with the intense luminosity of the limestone from which it is made.

◄ *Small head of Queen Tiy,* Berlin, Ägyptisches Museum, 21834. A double-plumed headdress was recently attributed to this piece. It shows a powerful woman, used to command. It dates from the end of the reign of Amenhotep III or that of Amenhotep IV, with all the characteristics of the latter period.

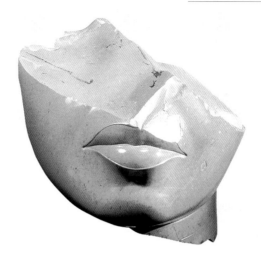

▼ *Statues of Amenhotep, son of Hapu,* Cairo, Egyptian Museum, CG 42127 and JE 44861. Amenhotep III's brilliant architect here has himself portrayed in an imitation of the austere style of the Middle Kingdom; but in accordance with the artistic canons of his time.

▲ *Fragment of a woman's face,* New York, The Metropolitan Museum of Art, 26.7.1396. The mouth is warmly sensual.

'Ka' statue of Amenhotep III

The temple of Luxor, much of which was built by Amenhotep III, was dedicated to the cult of the *ka*, a kind of double of the king. This sculpture is a very fine example (Luxor, Museum of Egyptian Art).

◀ The sledge indicates that the sculpture depicts the *ka* of the king, which is intangible and can be represented only in the form of a statue.

▼ *Head of Amenhotep III*, Cleveland, Museum of Art, 52.513. Late statues of Amenhotep often show him with the features of a child.

◀ The *ka* of Amenhotep III is a statue of a statue, with an adult's body and girlish features to signify that this form is unaffected by the passing of time. The childlike face complies with the artistic canons of the time, all of which were intended to emphasize beauty and perfection of line and form. This quartzite sculpture is one of the greatest masterpieces of Egyptian art.

▲ *Head of Amenhotep III,* Paris, Musée du Louvre, A 25. The blue crown, or *khepesh*, was first widely used in royal statuary during the reign of Amenhotep III.

▶ *Head of a colossal statue of Amenhotep III from his temple at Kom el-Hetan,* London, The British Museum, EA 7. In this sculpture, the quest for formal perfection is translated into simplified geometrical features.

The tomb of Ramose

ART AND ARCHITECTURE

The tomb of Ramose (TT 55) in Thebes is an extraordinary example of the sudden artistic changes which took place during the reigns of Amenhotep III and his son Akhenaten. The decoration of the pillared hall took a considerable time, and was therefore carried out using a variety of techniques; it was never completed. The east wall was decorated during the reign of Amenhotep III, using a very fine relief, with elegant scenes depicting members of Ramose's family. The upper part of the south wall, however, was painted with scenes of funeral ceremonies. The group of grief-stricken women is full of movement and pathos, and stands out within the formal simplicity of the rest of the scene.

The decoration of the west wall, which is incomplete, represents an uncompromising break with the other parts of the room. It shows Akhenaten receiving delegations of foreigners. The detached and precious formalism of a few years previously appears very distant in time compared with these uniquely powerful images.

▼ The people shown in the reliefs comply with the canons of beauty and purity which applied during the reign of Amenhotep III, and therefore have childlike, feminine features. The abundantly detailed clothing enriches the scenes by creating ripples of light.

◀ In the paintings of funeral scenes, the seriousness and immobility of the men contrasts with the realistically portrayed grief of the women, whose eye makeup is shown running.

◀ The curved backs of the officials bowing before Akhenaten are a departure from the usual canons, and give the scene a great deal of tension.

▼ The preparatory drawings from the Amarna Period show particular attention to detail in the facial features of the foreigners.

The Amarna Period

The ascent to the throne of Amenhotep IV, the son of Amenhotep III and Tiy, marked the beginning of a period of rapid and dramatic change in Egypt. Continuing the reforms begun by his father, the young king banned the cult of Amun-Ra and replaced it with that of Aten, the solar disc. At the same time he changed his own name to Akhenaten, meaning 'he who is useful to Aten'.

In the fifth year of his reign, in order to make his independence from Thebes more obvious, Akhenaten founded a new capital at El-Amarna in Middle Egypt, and transferred the whole of his court there. This move greatly accelerated the pace of cultural change, in which the past was rejected and the advent of a new era was heralded.

In art, there was a return to the styles of the previous period; formalism was taken to its extremes, and lines became fundamentally important. There was a growing interest in the events of everyday life. This resulted in a greater interest in movement and a different use of figurative space. This tendency is also seen in written texts, which take on a register of language close to the spoken language.

▲ *Statue of a queen or princess,* Paris, Musée du Louvre, E 25409. The female form has been accentuated to show its fertility, seemingly bursting out of the flimsy pleated robe whose transparency creates soft but intense contrasts of light along the body.

◀ *Painted limestone pair*, Paris, Musée du Louvre, E 15593. This little group was located in the chapel of a private house at El-Amarna. Akhenaten and his wife Nefertiti are portrayed in a very natural way, with a strikingly relaxed treatment of space; the fact that they are holding hands conveys a sense of calm intimacy.

◀ *Painted limestone sculptor's model of Nefertiti offering flowers to Akhenaten*, Berlin, Ägyptisches Museum, 15000. The informal arrangement of the figures within the scene is one of the main features of art during the reign of Akhenaten. The relaxed figure of the king is particularly striking, with a gust of wind blowing part of his robe into the air. The image of Nefertiti is more static, and the artist is more interested in the possibilities afforded by the colour and transparency of the robe. He has made the legs visible through it.

▼ *Painted relief*, Luxor, Museum of Egyptian Art, J 23. The decoration of Amenhotep IV's temple at Karnak depicts the hubbub of everyday life.

▼ *Akhenaten and the royal family*, Berlin, Ägyptisches Museum, 14145. Amarna art often shows royalty in everyday activities under Aten's rays.

Osiride pilaster of Akhenaten

The colossal effigy of Akhenaten (Cairo, Egyptian Museum, JE 49528) formed part of a statue engaged with a pilaster in the temple dedicated to Aten (Gempaaton), erected by the king to the east of the temple of Amun-Ra at Karnak during the early years of his reign.

▶ The small almond-shaped eyes, long, delicate nose, fleshy mouth and elongated chin are typical features of the vigorous, extreme style of the early Amarna Period.

◄ *Profiles of Akhenaten*, Cairo, Egyptian Museum, JE 59294. The two different profiles on a single slab of limestone show how the art of Amarna was constantly evolving.

▲ *Fragment from the top of a colossal statue of Akhenaten from the Gempaaton at Karnak*, Paris, Musée du Louvre, E 27112.

► *Sculptor's model*, Berlin, Ägyptisches Museum, 14512. The exaggerated features which give life to intensely hieratic colossal statues of Akhenaten are here almost a caricature.

▲ *Plaster head of Akhenaten*, Berlin, Ägyptisches Museum, 21348. This head was probably based on a statue made in the last years of Akhenaten's reign. The second phase of the Amarna Period was more meditative in style, without the overstatement of the early period.

81

The end of the Amarna Period

The winds of reform and innovation which blew through Egypt during the Amarna period ceased when Akhenaten died. He was succeeded first by Smenkhkara, who reigned only for a short time, and then by Tutankhamun, who came to the throne at the age of nine. It was during the latter's reign that a period of normalization began, leading to the restoration of the cult of Amun-Ra and a reversion to tradition, most obviously symbolized by the return of the court to Thebes. Artists stayed ahead of political and religious reforms; during the last few years of Akhenaten's reign they abandoned the extremes and exaggeration which had revolutionized Egyptian culture during the early Amarna Period.

◀ *Quartzite head of a princess*, Berlin, Ägyptisches Museum, 2123. This piece marks the maturity of Amarna art; although its forms are rather overstated, it lacks the exaggeration of the early period. The whole of the face is made up of harmonious curves, and the elongated oval of the skull has been placed on an elegant and graceful neck.

▲ *Unfinished statue of Akhenaten or Nefertiti kissing a princess*, Cairo, Egyptian Museum, JE 44866.

▼ *Upper part of a painted limestone statue of a princess*, Paris, Musée du Louvre, E 14715.

▲ *Stela of Bay*, Cairo, Egyptian Museum, JE 34177. Here a private person appropriates the Amarna style.

▼ *Ushabti*, private collection. In his ushabtis, Akhenaten is portrayed in a more simple and meditative way.

GREAT MASTERPIECES

The Berlin Nefertiti

The *Head of Nerfertiti* now in the Ägyptisches
Museum in Berlin (21300) was found together with many
other unfinished statues in the workshop of the sculptor
Djehutymes at El-Amarna (house P 47).

▲ The head has no
left eye because it
was never completed.
It probably served as
a model for sculptures
of the queen, whose
beauty is warmly and
realistically portrayed.

▼ *Statue of Nefertiti*, Berlin, Ägyptisches Museum, 21263. The intense facial features contrast strongly with the full, languid form of the body.

▶ *Head of Nefertiti*, Cairo, Egyptian Museum, JE 45547. Although it was found under the foundations of the palace of Merenptah at Memphis, this head of a queen undoubtedly portrays Nefertiti. It is probably one of the large number of statues in a variety of materials made during the Amarna Period.

▶ *Head of Nefertiti*, Cairo, Egyptian Museum, JE 59286. Despite being incomplete, this piece is typical of the balanced formalism of the mature Amarna style.

The end of the 18th dynasty

In the fifth year of the young Tutankhamun's reign, he and his court abandoned El-Amarna. The desert sands overran the 'Horizon of Aten', as the ancient city was called, and subsequent pharaohs and officials sought to erase every trace of Akhenaten and what his period had represented.

Figures of the god Amun-Ra were widely restored after the destruction wrought on them by followers of Aten. Artists gradually returned to the styles they had abandoned in their violent rejection of the artistic canons, in which they had used movement and naturalism to bring their work to life amid a framework of abstract formalism.

Something of this irrepressible force remained in the monuments of Akhenaten's immediate successors, albeit on a diminished scale. The heavy eyelids, almond eyes, fleshy lips and slightly bulging stomachs of Amarna portraits were echoed in the statues of the latter part of the dynasty. The process of restoration was completed by Horemheb, a general who succeeded the high priest Ay as the ruler of Egypt, though Akhenaten and his time had left an indelible mark.

▲ *Fragmentary painted quartzite statue of Tutankhamun from Medinet Habu,* Cairo, Egyptian Museum, JE 59869.

◀ The *mask of Tutankhamun* (Cairo, Egyptian Museum, JE 60672) owes its extraordinary fascination to the traces of Amarna art in a work based primarily on the clear and classical abstraction of previous periods.

◀ *Statue of Maya and Merit,* Leiden, Rijksmuseum van Oudheden, AST 1-3. The overall composition and the two figures' clothing recall sculpture from the period before Akhenaten's reign. However, the facial features are inspired by Amarna canons.

▼ *Statue of Horemheb kneeling before Atum,* Luxor, Museum of Egyptian Art. This unique sculpture shows King Horemheb making an offering to the god Atum of two small globe-shaped vases of water.

ART AND ARCHITECTURE

The tomb of Horemheb at Saqqara

Before becoming the last king of the 18th dynasty, Horemheb had been commander in chief of the Egyptian army under Tutankhamun. During his reign, when the influence of Amarna art was still very strong, he began building an imposing tomb in the sands of Saqqara. The original design was extended a number of times to reflect the general's growing importance within the court. It was then abandoned when Horemheb ascended the throne of Egypt and, like all his predecessors, he had a tomb complex built for himself in the Valley of the Kings.

The superstructure of his tomb at Saqqara looks like a small temple, and its interior is decorated with reliefs which still retain the vivid expressive force of the Amarna Period. The story of Horemheb's feats is recounted in highly dramatic and intensely realistic terms, with scenes of great pathos and movement verging on confusion, full of carefully drawn figures whose faces convey powerful emotions.

▲ *Relief depicting Egyptian soldiers advancing into the desert,* Bologna, Civico Museo Archeologico, KS 1889.

◀ *Relief depicting Nubian prisoners,* Bologna, Civico Museo Archeologico, KS 1887. The prisoners show the distinctive Nubian racial traits, but each one has individual features. The scene is given depth by depicting the figures in different planes and sizes.

◀ *Relief*, Leiden, Rijksmuseum van Oudheden, HIII.PPP, 999. The horses seem about to run away in terror.

▼ The face of the Syrian clearly shows his fear in the presence of the king. This intense emotion is underlined by the zigzag arrangement of the figures, as though they can hardly manage to stand upright.

▶ *Scene relating to Chapter 110 of the Book of the Dead*, Bologna, Civico Museo Archeologico, KS 1885. The scene uses illustrations copied from papyri, lacking the narrative tension of the other reliefs, and the style is very rigid and formal. Horemheb wears the royal *uraeus*, or rearing cobra, which was placed on his forehead when he became pharaoh.

Shrine for canopic jars

The *Shrine for canopic jars* (Cairo, Egyptian Museum, JE 60686), which forms part of the treasure of Tutankhamun, is the item which most clearly shows the complex artistic sensitivity of the post-Amarna Period.

▲ The shrine is made of wood covered in gold leaf. It consists of several pieces which have been assembled to create a delicate and balanced whole. The shrine itself is placed on runners, and has a canopy on top. The goddesses Isis, Nephthys, Neith and Selqet stand on the four sides with their arms protectively outstretched.

▲ The face of the scorpion goddess Selqet still shows traces of its proximity to the Amarna Period. The almond-shaped eyes and down-turned mouth recall the style of the latter part of Akhenaten's reign. The full body, with its clinging robe whose wide sleeves evoke the wings of the protecting goddesses, is endowed with movement by being slightly twisted. This is an unusual pose in Egyptian art, and confers an unexpected vitality on this gilded wooden statue.

▲ The container for canopic jars is divided into four compartments which hold the four jars containing the viscera of the dead person. The lid of each jar is in the shape of a bust of Tutankhamun. The young king is shown wearing the *nemes* headdress with the cobra and vulture representing the goddesses Wadjyt and Nekhbet, the protectors of Lower and Upper Egypt.

▼ The prominent features, careful formality and gentleness of Tutankhamun's face recall the style of the latter years of Akhenaten's reign.

▲ The container is made of alabaster inlaid with glass paste, and takes the form of a shrine on runners. Isis, Nephthys, Neith and Selqet appear again on the corners in low relief, their arms open as a sign of protection.

1550-1075 BC

The beginnings of the 19th dynasty

Since Horemheb did not have any direct heirs, he nominated Paramessu, a companion in arms from the Delta, to succeed him.

Paramessu was already advanced in years when he ascended the throne under the name of Rameses I. He in turn was succeeded by his son Sety I, who reclaimed Egypt's role as a world power after its loss during the second half of the 18th dynasty. He began an imposing programme of construction at Abydos, probably with the intention of legitimizing his own family by tracing its origins to Osiris, the king of the dead and mythical forerunner of all the kings of Egypt.

The religious complex dedicated to Osiris included a large temple and an underground cenotaph, the Osireion, which used a megalithic structure surrounded by water to represent the Delta, where according to legend Osiris had been buried.

▲ *Sety I offering to the goddess Maat, from the temple of Abydos.* In this painted relief, Sety is shown with a slightly hooked nose and full, oval face. The features recall those of the Thutmosid kings, and represent a rejection of the Amarna style.

Art continued to regress as the desire to return to tradition became increasingly evident. The modelling of figures recalled that of the first part of the 18th dynasty, but there was also a renewed interest in abundant detail and the elaborate play of light on surfaces. The painted reliefs of the time showed a tendency towards abstract perfection, which was achieved using poised forms and simple but sophisticated decoration of incomparable beauty.

◄ *Sety I and the goddess Hathor,* Paris, Musée du Louvre, B 7. Sety I's tomb is one of the biggest in the Valley of the Kings. It consists of two separate sections along a single axis, following the design inaugurated by Horemheb. The clear division into two parts refers to the dual destiny awaiting the king in the underworld. The upper level represents his celestial rebirth (in connection with the god Ra-Horakhty), while the lower one links him to Osiris and the underworld. The walls of the tomb are decorated with very high-quality painted reliefs which are elegantly modelled in brilliant colours, making the figures even more striking by bringing out the details and the transparency of their clothing.

▼ *Statuette of Sety I from Abydos,* Cairo, Egyptian Museum, CG 751. Despite lacking its lower half, this little sculpture is a paradigm for the whole of Ramesside art, and Sety I's face is the prototype for subsequent royal portraits.

The facial features are inspired by the Thutmosid tradition, but the influence of Amarna art is still apparent in the finely pleated clothing, which creates an elaborate play of light across the whole surface of the sculpture.

▲ *Colossal alabaster statue of Sety I,* Cairo, Egyptian Museum, CG 42139. This was made in various materials; the

modelling of the face suggests a work from a previous period usurped by Sety I, who added his own name to it.

Art as royal propaganda

The Ramesside royal chancellery used every means at its disposal to propagate the image of a just and powerful king with no rivals. In the areas of temples accessible to the public, the immense walls were used to recount his extraordinary feats, in crowded reliefs of battle and hunting scenes with the emphasis on the tangled, severed limbs of dead enemies or animals.

The king's greatness and uniqueness are expressed by showing him on a larger scale than the other figures, and separate from them. The contrast between his clearly-delineated and very visible image and the confusion of his opponents also serves to remind us of the eternal struggle between order and chaos, in which only the pharaoh can provide well-being and equilibrium.

From the reign of Sety I onwards, reliefs rapidly evolved into a narrative resource of extraordinary breadth. Some of the most dramatic examples depict the battle between Rameses II and the Hittites at Qadesh. These were incised on the walls of six temples built by the king, and compress the events of the battle into a single event so that the main outlines of the story can be understood without reading the text.

▲ *Sety I attacking the city of Qadesh,* northern outer wall of the Hypostyle Hall at Karnak. The difference in size between the horses pulling the royal chariot and the enemy troops serves to emphasize the king's power and greatness.

◄ *Rameses III hunting wild bulls,* first pylon of the temple of Medinet Habu.

▼ *The Egyptian encampment being attacked by the Hittites.* The story of the battle of Qadesh exalts the greatness of Rameses II and condemns the vile behaviour of the Hittites, who set out to win the day by attacking the Egyptian army without warning. The scene emphasizes this by showing two separate events from the story which occurred close together. The Egyptian soldiers are on the left, going about their daily tasks and unaware that the Hittites' chariots are approaching from the right, and the relief conveys a strong sense of impending tragedy.

▼ *Fragment of painted relief depicting slaughtered enemies,* New York, The Metropolitan Museum of Modern Art, 13.180.21. This comes from the funerary temple of Rameses IV.

▼ *Rameses II massacring the enemy beneath the walls of Qadesh,* detail from the battle scene sculpted on the west wall of the second pylon of the Ramesseum at Thebes.

95

Rameses II and the Ramesside Period

At sixty-six years, the reign of Rameses II was one of the longest in pharaonic history. Rameses continued the policies of his father Sety I, consolidating Egyptian power in the Near East and glorifying the role of royalty in a process which, after many centuries, restored divine status to the pharaoh. Art concluded its return to tradition which had been so strongly manifested during the time of Sety I, and it lost much of its tension and elegance.

This trend was more apparent in reliefs than in statuary, and some of the sculptures of this period display great artistic virtuosity; but two-dimensional art was used as propaganda to glorify the king's achievements and the new ideology of pharaonic royalty. Meaning became more important than form, and size and quantity more important than quality. Every work of art was a symbol designed to promote the message that the king was superhuman.

Architecture served a similar purpose. Temple walls became giant hoardings which used text and reliefs to celebrate Rameses II's greatness, and this was later bolstered by innumerable colossal statues.

▲ *Horus statue to Rameses II,* Cairo, Egyptian Museum, JE 64735. This statue can be interpreted as meaning 'Horus (the falcon god) protects Rameses II', and is an example of how every Ramesside work of art was designed to convey a message about royalty. The king's name is made up of that of the solar disc (*Ra*) and the head of a boy (*mes*) holding a rush (*su*).

◄ *Jubilee ceremony from a tomb at Saqqara,* Cairo, Egyptian Museum, JE 4872. Non-official Ramesside art remained more lively and full of movement.

▶ *Painted limestone statue of a Ramesside princess,* Cairo, Egyptian Museum, CG 600.

◀ The tomb of Queen Nefertari, the favourite wife of Rameses II, is one of the most beautiful funerary monuments of the Ramesside era. The low-relief decoration is painted in lively colours, but despite their beauty the figures are static, in common with all art of the period. The images of the gods, which were now part of a long-established tradition, contrast with that of the queen, who wears the elaborately pleated and transparent vestments that were in vogue at the time.

▼ *Painted granite statue,* Cairo, Egyptian Museum, CG 607. Rameses II was succeeded by his son Merenptah, who is depicted in this sculpture.

The Turin Rameses II

*B*lack granite statue of Rameses II, Turin, Museo Egizio, C 1380. An undisputed masterpiece of Egyptian statuary, embodying the idea of royalty during the Ramesside era.

◀ The statue shows the newly crowned king with a slightly downcast gaze, conveying a sense of intimacy and expressing his willingness to listen to his subjects' supplications. The right arm and sceptre extend beyond the bounds of the figure, creating a feeling of movement and accentuating the vibrancy of the pleated clothing that was fashionable at the time. This gives the statue an unexpected feeling of reality.

▲ *Fragment of a statue of Rameses II from Tanis,* Cairo, Egyptian Museum, JE 616. The wig creates a greater contrast between light and shade than in the Turin Rameses.

▼ *Head of Rameses II,* Rome, Museo Barracco, 21. In this head, the influence of Amarna art is still apparent in the blue crown, narrow eyes and heavy eyebrows.

▲ *Head of a colossal statue of Rameses II,* London, The British Museum, EA 19. The larger size makes this image of the king more abstract and remote from everyday life.

ART AND ARCHITECTURE

The Abu Simbel temple complex

Abu Simbel, a few dozen kilometres from the southern boundary of Egypt, marked the completion of the process of royal glorification begun by Sety I and continued by his son Rameses II. After centuries, Rameses had succeeded in restoring divine status to the role of the king.

The Great Temple affirms this dogma by deliberately exploiting the ambiguity created by the combination of sculpture and hieroglyphs, and the Lesser Temple also expresses it by associating Nefertari with the cult of Hathor.

From an artistic point of view, the Great Temple reflects the desire to attract attention that was typical of all 19th-dynasty art. Although cut into the rock, its sheer grandeur and internal layout are an imitation of a normal built temple. It has the classic sloping structure, in which the rooms become smaller, the floors higher and the ceilings lower as the visitor approaches the cella, or inner chamber. The statues of the great Egyptian divinities are sculpted into the far wall of this last room, where Rameses rubs shoulders with Ptah, Amun-Ra and Ra-Horakhty.

The Lesser Temple has a simpler structure similar to that of a rock-cut chapel. The first room, in which the pillars are sculpted with the emblems of the goddess Hathor, leads into a transverse area providing direct access to the cella.

▲ The colossi of the Great Temple portray Rameses II as a sovereign whose face expresses the satisfaction of immeasurable power.

▼ The façade of the Great Temple recalls the entrance pylon of a built temple. The image of Ra-Horakhty above the entrance can be read as a rebus of Rameses II's name.

▲ The Hypostyle Hall of the Great Temple imitates the court of a built temple. The pillars dividing the room into three naves bear colossal figures of the king with all the insignia of power, as though enveloped in a robe which also covers his feet.

▲ The plan and section of the Great Temple clearly show the graduated structure of the rooms.

▼ The façade of the Lesser Temple is decorated with two statues of Nefertari and four of Rameses II cut into the rock.

The one on the far left is larger, as though indicating the direction of the temple dedicated to the king.

The end of the New Kingdom

With the exception of Sethnakhte, the founder of the 20th dynasty, all of its kings chose names based on that of Rameses II, whose memory also inspired the art of the time. Architecture still sought to impress, but with a greater monumentality of form. In his temple at Medinet Habu, Rameses III used the same general layout as the Ramesseum (the temple built by to Rameses II on the west bank at Thebes), and also copied some of its decorations, but with exaggerated proportions. However, the result has none of the vitality and desire to impress that was typical of all art of the previous period. Statuary and two-dimensional decoration showed the same tendency towards imitation, though they lacked the grandeur of the early 19th dynasty.

On the other hand, the royal tombs of this time were monumental and flamboyant. The tomb-artists made sketches of an informal kind, found all around the village of Deir el-Medina where they lived. These *ostraca* capture the essence of the Rameside Period, their rapid brushstrokes portraying in sometimes entertaining fashion a changing society in which Egyptians were becoming aware both of their own individuality, and of the existence of a world outside the Nile valley.

▲ *Granite statue of Rameses III with standard of Amun,* Cairo, Egyptian Museum, JE 42150. Statues bearing emblems of divinities were common throughout the Rameside era.

◀ *The family of Inherkhau, from his tomb at Deir el-Medina* (TT 359). In the decoration of their own tombs, the workers who had built the tombs in the Valley of the Kings adopted a style very different from the official canons, as evinced by this lively scene showing the dead man and his wife surrounded by their children.

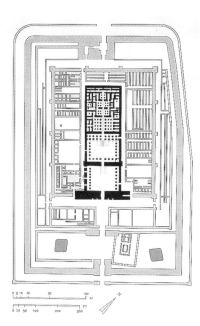

▲ Plan of the temple of Rameses III at Medinet Habu. The central structure is surrounded by a series of unfired mud-brick buildings used as offices and stores.

▼ The first pylon of the temple of Rameses III at Medinet Habu. The building is directly inspired by the temple of Rameses II a few kilometres away.

▲ The entrance gate to Medinet Habu. An unfired mud-brick wall surrounded the sacred area, and the gates were inspired by the fortified entrances to cities in the Near East.

▼ *Granite statue of Ramessunakht,* Cairo, Egyptian Museum, CG 42162. The baboon is the scribe's god Thoth, under whose protection Ramessunakht is placed.

Ramesside *ostraca*

*O*straca are fragments of limestone or pots used by artists to make notes or draw sketches. Egyptian scribes used these to express themselves in ways which did not comply with the official artistic canons.

▲ *Ostracon depicting a dancer*, Turin, Museo Egizio, C 7052. The long, rapid lines and the contrast between the pale body and black hair and loincloth make this a masterpiece of delicate grace and vivacity.

◄ *Paris ostracon*, Paris, Musée du Louvre, E 14366. Here, the hyena's terrified immobility contrasts with the furious motion of the excited dogs.

◀ *Ostracon depicting wrestlers*, Cairo, Egyptian Museum, CG 25139. The two figures have first been outlined in red and then finished in black. The difference in height between them, and their powerful musculature, suggests that the scene may have been based on the observation of reality. The artist has ignored all the artistic conventions and used the means at his disposal to capture the tension of the two men eyeing each other.

◀ *Ostracon depicting the queen of Punt*, Berlin, Ägyptisches Museum, ÄS 21442. This quick sketch is a version of the relief in Hatshepsut's temple at Deir el-Bahri.

▲ *Ostracon depicting a king in profile*, Paris, Musée du Louvre, N 498. The accurate rendering of facial detail has made this into a lively piece of caricature.

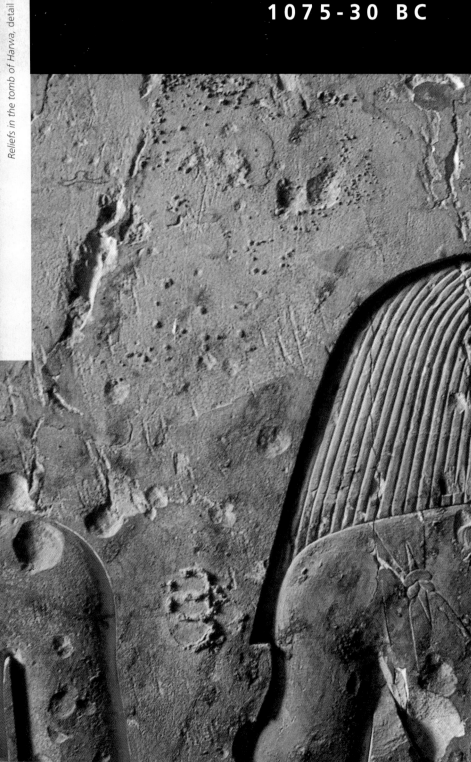

Reliefs in the tomb of Harwa, detail

The Third Intermediate Period

The fragmentation of Egypt during the late New Kingdom led to the development of two different artistic styles. The northern state continued to take its inspiration from the forms and styles of the Ramesside monarchical tradition, in an attempt to perpetuate its glory. The practice whereby kings attributed the works of their predecessors to themselves by adding their own names became very widespread. Tanis, the royal residence in the 21st and 22nd dynasties, was adorned with monuments dating almost exclusively from the Ramesside era, taken from various locations in Lower Egypt. However, the grave goods in metal and precious stones found in the royal tombs at Tanis are more original. These Near Eastern-influenced pieces are very fine examples of metalware, despite their less finished style.

The art which began to grow up in the south during this period was more distinctive. Isolated from Mediterranean influences and seeking to affirm its own ancient origins, the Theban priestly aristocracy began developing a taste for the archaic, and this became widespread from the 25th dynasty onwards.

◀ *Fragment of a sandstone statue of Osorkon I,* Paris, Musée du Louvre, AO 9502. Osorkon I has appropriated a Ramesside statue simply by having his own name carved on its chest. The Phoenician inscription is that of King Elibaal of Byblos, where the sculpture was found.

▼ *Painted limestone statue of Osorkon III,* Cairo, Egyptian Museum, CG 42197. The king is shown kneeling and presenting a boat to the god.

▼ *Graywacke statue of a queen*, Berlin, Ägyptisches Museum, ÄS 10114. The facial features are markedly Ramesside in style, but the simple modelling of the clothes indicates that the piece dates from a later period.

▲ *Osorkon II's gold and lapis lazuli triad from Abydos*, Paris, Musée du Louvre, E 6204. The small effigies of Osiris, Isis and Horus reveal the artistic skill of goldsmiths of the time.

▶ *Granite statue of the vizier Hor*, Cairo, Egyptian Museum, JE 37512. The pose is inspired by statues from the Old Kingdom, but the contrast between smooth and inscribed surfaces, and the bald head and idealized features reflect the artistic canons of the Third Intermediate Period.

Statuette of the divine adoratrice Karomama

*S*tatuette *of the divine adoratrice Karomama*, Paris, Musée du Louvre, N 500. This bronze figure of a priestess is an extraordinary example of the virtuosity attained by Egyptian metalworkers during the Third Intermediate Period.

◄ Karomama is depicted in the full flower of youth. The heavy wig and short-sleeved robe emphasize the graceful face and well-proportioned body. A touch of sensuality is conferred upon the figure by the measured gait, rich decoration and damascened robes, which accentuate the female form rather than concealing it. Although the sculpture is inspired by models from the Ramesside period, it is more graceful.

◀ *Statue of Meresamun,* Berlin, Ägyptisches Museum, ÄS 71/71. The slight smile is an artistic convention of the Third Intermediate Period, while the prominent breasts anticipate the style of subsequent periods.

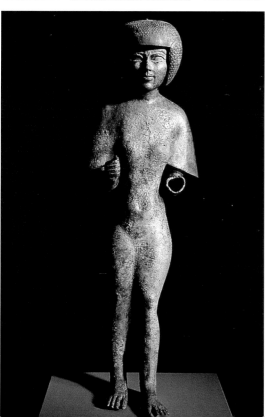

◀ *Statuette of a priestess,* Leiden, Rijksmuseum van Oudheden. Although the pose is similar to that of Karomama, this statuette serves a different artistic purpose and places greater emphasis on the naturalistic rendering of the female body, at the expense of the lightness and grace of the Louvre masterpiece.

111

HISTORIC AND ARTISTIC CONTEXT

The 25th dynasty and the return to the ancient style

The fragmented political situation in Egypt at the end of the New Kingdom led to the creation of an autonomous Kushite kingdom in Nubia. The Kushite king, Piankhy, exploited the weakness of the northern states by annexing Upper Egypt and placing the kings of the Delta under his influence, thus creating the 25th dynasty.

During almost a century of Kushite dominion, there was a return to an older style inspired primarily by the art of the Middle Kingdom. This renaissance had its centre at Thebes, where there had already been sporadic signs of a return to the courtly styles and forms of the past during the previous period. This was accompanied in private statuary by greater characterization of physical features. Although portraits of kings became more abstract, they still bore the typically Nubian racial features.

◀ *Granodiorite head of Taharqo*, Aswan, Museum of Nubian Civilization, CG 560. In this piece, references to older models are apparent within the more heavy style typical of this period.

▲ Much building took place at Karnak during the 25th dynasty. This block, which was reused in a later building, bears a relief inspired by the strong and decisive style of the late 11th dynasty.

▼ *Gold, silver and bronze statuette of Taharqo worshipping the falcon god Hemen,* Paris, Musée du Louvre, E 25676. This is a rare example of the very fine work in precious metals of the time.

▲▼ *Statues of Montuemhat,* Cairo, Egyptian Museum, CG 42236 and 647. Montuemhat, a late 25th-dynasty vizier, displays his knowledge of the past by having himself portrayed in statues inspired by various earlier periods in Egyptian art.

ART AND ARCHITECTURE

The tomb of Harwa

▲ The style of the reliefs in Harwa's tomb recalls that of the Old Kingdom, though here the facial features are more distinct.

Harwa held senior office in the priesthood of Amun-Ra in Thebes between the late 8th and early 7th centuries BC. He was responsible for governing the southern territories of Egypt on behalf of the Kushite kings, and this entitled him to build himself a huge tomb on the level ground of El Assasif, right opposite the temple of Mentuhotep II at Deir el-Bahri.

Harwa was the first person in nearly three hundred years to carry out such a large project, and its size is closer to that of the tombs in the Valley of the Kings than those of dignitaries during the previous period. His example was followed by other Theban officials who built their tombs around his, copying its main decorative and architectural features and thus acknowledging its importance and the fact that it had been built before theirs.

Harwa's tomb (TT 37) consists of a number of underground levels, and its rooms are arranged in imitation of the ideal layout of Osiris' tomb. Architecture, text and decoration are used as competing means of communicating messages relating to life, death, and survival in the underworld. The return to the ancient style which characterized the whole period is reflected in the abstract and carefully thought-out beauty of the reliefs.

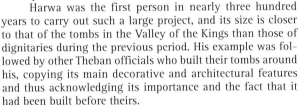

◄ *Anubis leading Harwa into the underworld.* Here, the Egyptian artist has managed to convey in stone the sadness of the moment of death.

▶ The end wall of the room, which concludes the series of areas along the main axis, contains a small high-relief image of Osiris. From a distance it looks bigger than it really is, forming the final focus of an unexpected *trompe-l'oeil*.

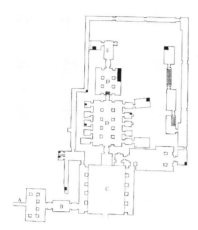

▲ A corridor surrounds the central underground section of the tomb, isolating it from the surrounding area and symbolically recalling the island in the Delta on which, according to myth, Isis buried Osiris.

The areas along the main axis gradually become narrower, as in a temple. The well in the second pillared hall leads into a series of rooms (not visible on the plan) which imitate the descent into hell.

▲ *Ushabti of Harwa.* The modelling of this ushabti figure recalls the artistic canons of the Old Kingdom.

The 26th dynasty and the Egyptian renaissance

The period of Kushite dominion was brought to an end by the Assyrian sacking of Thebes in 664 BC. Egypt once again became independent, under a dynasty of kings from Sais in the western Delta. In order to assert the legitimacy of their claim to the throne of the pharaohs, the Saitic kings advocated a return to ancient culture and presented this as a veritable Egyptian renaissance.

Although this trend was apparent from the beginning of the dynasty and was not a continuation of what the Kushite kings had done before, the re-evaluation of ancient culture became a major phenomenon only during the reign of Amasis. Art moved towards abstraction, placing an even greater emphasis on geometric purity of form. Statues were made from extremely hard stone which could be used to create smooth, luminous surfaces. The slight smile on the faces of this period later became one of the characteristics of archaic Greek sculpture.

▲ *Head of Amasis*, Berlin, Ägyptisches Museum, 11864.

◀ *Head of Amasis*, Baltimore, Walters Art Gallery, 22.415. Amasis was elected pharaoh by the army which had rebelled against Apries. He gave privileges to foreign mercenaries and allowed Greeks and Cypriots to found the trading city of Naukratis in the Delta, which soon became a cultural conduit between Egypt and the Aegean.

The two heads portray Amasis with idealized but unmistakable features, even though they have differently shaped oval faces.

▶ *Block statue of Iahmes, son of Pakharkhonsu,* Cairo, Egyptian Museum, JE 36579. The block statue remained highly popular throughout Egyptian history. During the Saitic period, its closed geometric structure became even more abstract, and tended to enclose the shape of the body within a rigidly symmetrical framework.

▲ *Toeris,* Cairo, Egyptian Museum, CG 39194. The monstrous appearance of the goddess is almost completely negated by the simple purity of this magnificent sculpture.

▼ *Funeral ceremony from the tomb of Nespaqashuty* (TT 312), New York, Brooklyn Museum of Art, 52.131.3. The Saitic artist has expressed the intense sorrow of death in a chaotic scene dominated by the convulsive movement of the mourners' raised arms. The drama and emotion of this scene is unparalleled among the art of its time.

1075-30 BC

Statue of the vizier Nespaqashuty

Statue of the vizier Nespaqashuty, Cairo, Egyptian Museum, JE 36665. This graywacke sculpture, a Saite masterpiece, is inspired by Old-Kingdom statues of scribes.

◄ The statue is striking in its extreme splendour and perfectly geometric surfaces, turning the human form into a set of striking abstract forms. The exaggeration of the hips, which are joined to the forearms, suggests that the work is meant to be viewed from the front.

▲ *Limestone statue of a scribe,* Paris, Musée du Louvre, E 3023 (5th dynasty).

▲ *Statue of Ptashepses,* Cairo, Egyptian Museum, CG 83. This 5th-dynasty limestone statue typically depicts a scribe writing on papyrus.

▶ *Granite statue of Petamenophis,* Cairo, Egyptian Museum, JE 37341. At the height of the 7th century BC, Petamenophis had himself portrayed as a scribe in a pose dating from almost two thousand years earlier.

The first Persian domination

In 525 BC, the troops of Cambyses II routed the Egyptian army at Pelusium and reduced the Nile valley to a satrapy, or province, of the immense Achaemenid empire. Before pacifying the region completely, Cambyses had to put down a bloody revolt during which he occupied Memphis. Many members of the Egyptian ruling classes were executed, and others were deported to Persia. These events gave the Achaemenid kings an evil reputation, though under a policy inaugurated by Cyrus II they sought to gain recognition from the Egyptians.

Like other peoples in subsequent periods, the Persians were fascinated by Egyptian culture and drew inspiration from it. Their winged god Ahura-Mazda was identified with the local sun god, and they also adopted some aspects of Egyptian art. In architecture, for example, the Persians used the layout and some of the characteristic features of Egyptian religious buildings.

These influences also worked in the opposite direction, and Achaemenid rule brought a number of changes in the style of Egyptian art. This is most obvious in statuary; although sculptors continued using the style, forms and types of the 26th dynasty, they began showing a real interest in the realistic portrayal of the face.

▲ *Headless statue of Darius I,* Teheran, Iran Bastan Museum. Found at Susa in Iran, this statue was undoubtedly made in Egypt. The king is shown in the classic walking pose, wearing Persian dress. The folds of his robe bear dense inscriptions in hieroglyphs, Elamite and Old Persian.

◀ *Statue of a falcon god,* Munich, Bayerische Landesbank. The use of silver, which was rare in Egypt, and various stylistic details, indicate that this piece was possibly made in Persia.

◀ *Upper section of a graywacke statue of an unknown man*, Paris, Musée du Louvre, N 2454. The slight smile and abstract facial features of Saitic art have given way to a realistically frowning mouth and obvious signs of age around the eyes.

▼ *Psammeticus Saneith holding a shrine (naophoros)*, Cairo, Egyptian Museum, CG 726. This type of statue became popular from the 26th dynasty onwards.

▼ The oasis of Kharga, on the edges of the Persian empire, served as a trading post and resting place for caravans heading for Nubia. Darius I built here the temple of Hibis, dedicated to the god Amun. Persian architecture was influenced by that of Egypt, and Darius' palace at Susa is similar to an Egyptian religious building, with distinctive features including gutters, capitals decorated with plant motifs, and architraves with winged solar discs.

The last native dynasties

The history of Egypt during the 4th century BC is one of continuous conflict with the Persians. Various kings in the Delta managed to gain recognition as pharaohs for brief periods, thanks mainly to alliances with Greek cities or to rebellions in other regions of the vast Achaemenid empire. The Persians managed to occupy the Delta in 343 BC despite strong resistance, beginning a short period of domination which ended with the arrival of Alexander the Great.

There are few monuments documenting the art and architecture of this troubled century. A fairly significant amount of construction took place during the 30th dynasty, when strong nationalism led artists to return to the forms of previous periods. The works of Nectanebo I and II, the first and third kings of the dynasty, were inspired mainly by the 26th dynasty. Reliefs began including large empty spaces interspersed with graceful figures pared down to their essentials. A similar trend occurred in sculpture, where there was a renewed preference for stylized abstraction rather than physiognomy.

▲ *Egg-shaped head*, Berlin, Ägyptisches Museum, 8805. This represents a type which became widespread in private statuary from the 27th dynasty onwards.

◀ In this statue (New York, The Metropolitan Museum of Art, 34.2.1), the carefully realised figure of the king contrasts with the stylized falcon. The sculpture can also be seen as a rebus representing the name of Nectanebo.

◀ *Sculptor's model for figure of a king,* Milan, Civiche Raccolte Archeologiche, E 0.9.40015. Objects like this have been variously dated to between the 26th dynasty and the Ptolemaic Period. They consist of limestone slabs on which Egyptian artists practised by copying a variety of subjects. In this case, the sculptor has carved a bust of a king with a blue crown. The piece is clearly modelled on a statue, since the shoulder has been made in full profile. The accurate modelling, with its attractively flat and smooth surfaces, dates it to a period between the 30th dynasty and the early Ptolemaic Period.

▼ *Frieze depicting figures bearing offerings,* Cairo, Egyptian Museum, JE 46591. Part of the decoration in the tomb of Horhotep, a priest at Buto, this scene is clearly influenced by 26th-dynasty models.

▲ *Lion attacking a calf,* Vienna, Kunsthistorisches Museum, 8020. Many 30th-dynasty statues of lions have survived, but this is the only one to show the lion in action, using an iconography that was very widespread in the Near East.

The tomb of Petosiris at Tuna el-Gebe

The family tomb of Petosiris, the high priest of Thoth, is located at Hermopolis in Middle Egypt and dates from the early Ptolemaic dynasty. Its decoration reflects the confluence between Egyptian art and the nascent Hellenistic style.

▲ The small shrine above the funerary shaft of Petosiris' tomb has been made in imitation of a classic Egyptian temple. The façade has four columns with composite capitals whose decoration recalls rich floral motifs. The intercolumnar slabs bear traditional-style scenes showing Petosiris making offerings to Thoth, the god of writing and patron of Hermopolis. They demonstrate the priest's important role within the city, since he is depicted in a manner normally reserved for kings.

◀ Bearers of offerings. The hall before the funeral chapel is decorated with reliefs which draw on the Egyptian funerary repertoire (as here), but are in the Hellenistic style. A wealth of decorative elements fills the spaces between the figures.

◀ *Harvest scene.* This theme has a long tradition in the decoration of Egyptian tombs. In that of Petosiris, the position of the figures (with the child between the two adults) appears to have been taken from New-Kingdom Theban tombs, while the figures themselves are clearly inspired by contemporary Hellenistic models.

◀ *Grape-picking scene.* The clothing and physiognomy of the peasants in this scene show clear and strong Hellenistic influences. The vine tendrils filling all the empty spaces are a complex and elaborate form of decoration, showing that this new form of art had little in common with traditional Egyptian art apart from the themes it dealt with.

▶ *The cobra goddess Wadjyt and the vulture goddess Nekhbet protecting the god Osiris with their wings.* Reliefs on religious and funerary themes are in the traditional Egyptian style, as in this scene, where Osiris is shown as a scarab in the centre.

Egyptian art in the Ptolemaic Period

Alexander the Great's conquest and the foundation of Alexandria marked the beginning of a process which led to the coexistence of native and Greek cultures in the Nile valley. This duality persisted throughout the Ptolemaic Period, which saw the Macedonian royal house ruling over a proud Egyptian population that was strongly attached to its own traditions.

There is, therefore, little continuity between the art of the 30th dynasty and that of the early Ptolemaic Period. Egyptian artists throughout the Nile valley continued to be influenced by the styles and models of past periods, seeking to keep their cultural identity as intact as possible. At the same time, Greek artists in workshops in Alexandria were making royal sculptures in the more classical Graeco-Macedonian tradition.

The contact between the two schools was manifested in works which, although totally Egyptian in style, included typically Greek attributes, hairstyles, or details of clothing. It was also reflected in a greater interest in the male portrait, which led to the creation of some very fine sculptures.

▲ *Upper part of the statue of Horsatutu,* Berlin, Ägyptisches Museum, 2271. The strongly individualized face and the clothing in the Greek style are grafted onto the Egyptian character of the sculpture.

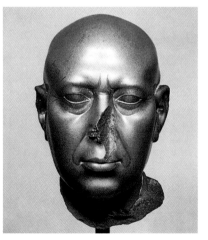

◀ *Berlin Green Head,* Berlin, Ägyptisches Museum, 12500. Private statuary of this period continued to use models from ancient pharaonic times, such as the block statue and the *naophoros* (shrine-holding statue). However, faces acquired more characterization, especially in the many highly expressive heads of elderly men such as this famous and superlative piece sculpted from very fine-grained schist. The features are enormously powerful and minutely detailed. The work has been dated to the 3rd century BC, and despite its entirely Egyptian style, shows the Greek interest in the depiction of anatomy.

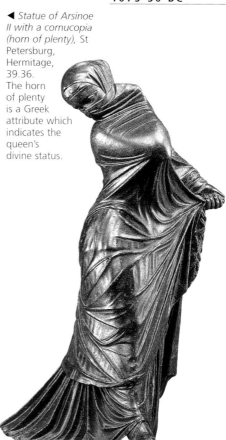

◀ *Statue of Arsinoe II with a cornucopia (horn of plenty)*, St Petersburg, Hermitage, 39.36. The horn of plenty is a Greek attribute which indicates the queen's divine status.

◀ *Ptolemy V*, New York, Brooklyn Museum of Art, 54.68. The head has been identified as Ptolemy V on the basis of the distinctive shape of the face. Ptolemy was only five years old when he came to the throne, and has therefore been portrayed as an adolescent. During his reign, royal statuary reverted to the style of the classical Egyptian tradition.

▲ *Statuette of a dancer*, New York, The Metropolitan Museum of Art, Walter Baker donation. Although statuettes of women dancing have been found throughout the Greek world, the characteristics of this very fine bronze example suggest that it was made in Alexandria. The statuette concentrates on the dancer's harmonious movement and transparent clothing.

Ptolemaic temples

Many of the temples built during the Ptolemaic Period were designed to meet the needs of an increasingly self-absorbed priesthood which used religious buildings to perpetuate its own ancient traditions. As a result, many existing temples were wholly or partly dismantled and rebuilt to emphasize the separation between external chaos and internal order.

▲ The temple of Isis at Philae, seen from the west.

Although this was done in various ways in response to particular religious needs (such as the double Holy of Holies in the temple of Kom Ombo, dedicated to Horus and Sobek), or to geographical factors (as on the island of Philae), Ptolemaic temples followed the same plan. They were inspired by earlier religious buildings, which resulted in a gradual decrease in the amount of space and light. Walls were covered in densely packed hieroglyphic texts and scenes depicting myths, rituals and festivals. The arrangement of both script and figures shows a *horror vacui* which also led to a very detailed rendering of clothing. Bodies were full, and faces idealized.

◀ The temple of the god Horus at Edfu has the typical Ptolemaic plan: a monumental gateway (pylon) leads to a court. The sanctuary is reached via a series of halls.

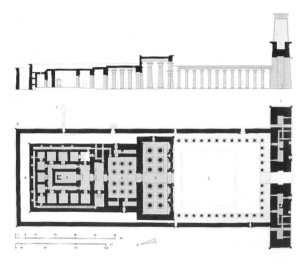

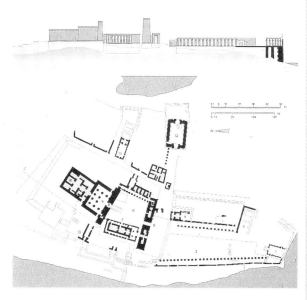

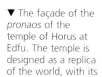

▶ The temple complex dedicated to Isis on the island of Philae underwent many expansions, some of them during the period of Roman rule. One included the colonnades which precede the first pylon.

▼ The façade of the *pronaos* of the temple of Horus at Edfu. The temple is designed as a replica of the world, with its columns decorated with plant motifs and ceilings representing the heavens.

▼ Monolithic *naos* inside the Holy of Holies of the temple of Horus at Edfu. Its doors were opened in the morning for the various ceremonies held throughout the day to worship the statue.

List of kings in the 'corridor of the kings' in the temple of Sety I at Abydos (detail)

Map of ancient Egypt

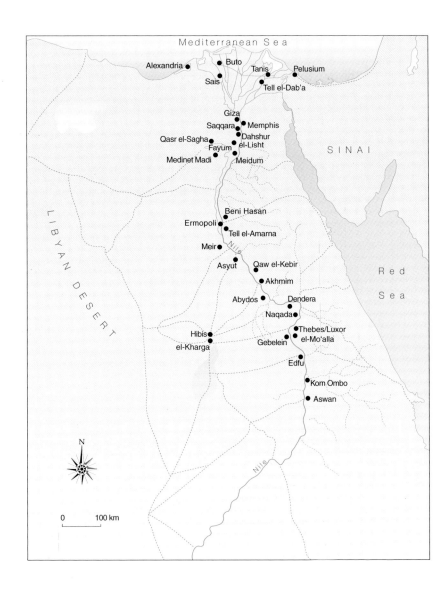

Mediterranean Sea

Alexandria
Buto
Sais
Tanis
Pelusium
Tell el-Dab'a

Giza
Saqqara
Memphis
Qasr el-Sagha
Dahshur
Fayum
el-Lisht
Medinet Madi
Meidum

SINAI

Beni Hasan
Ermopoli
Tell el-Amarna
Meir
Nile
Asyut
Qaw el-Kebir
Akhmim
Abydos
Dendera
Naqada

Red
Sea

LIBYAN DESERT

Hibis
Thebes/Luxor
el-Kharga
Gebelein
el-Mo'alla
Edfu
Kom Ombo
Aswan

N

0   100 km

Nile

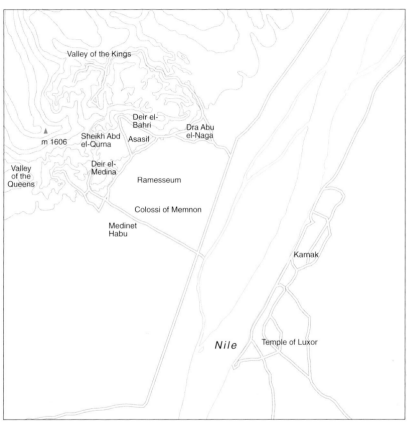

Valley of the Kings

Deir el-Bahri

Dra Abu el-Naga

m 1606

Sheikh Abd el-Qurna

Asasif

Valley of the Queens

Deir el-Medina

Ramesseum

Colossi of Memnon

Medinet Habu

Karnak

Nile

Temple of Luxor

◄ *Map of Egypt under the pharaohs.* This shows only those sites mentioned in the text, and ignores chronological differences.

▲ *Map of the Thebes/Luxor area.* The temples and settlement were built on the east bank of the Nile, and the necropolises and funerary temples on the west bank.

Chronology

▶ *Statue of Senusret III*, New York, Brooklyn Museum, 52.1.

Regnal dates are given only for kings mentioned in the text.

Predynastic period
(4000-3000 BC)

Naqada I culture
(4000-3500 BC)
Naqada II (3500-3100)

Dynasty 0 (c. 3000)
Narmer

▼ *Statue of Khufu*, Cairo, Egyptian Museum, JE 36143.

Early Dynastic Period
(2920-2575 BC)

1st dynasty (2920-2770)
Djet
Qa'a

2nd dynasty (2770-2650)
Khasekhemwy

3rd dynasty (2650-2575)
Djoser (Netjerkhet) 2630-2611

Old Kingdom (2575-2135)

4th dynasty (2575-2465)
Sneferu 2575-2551
Khufu 2551-2528
Djedefra 2528-2520
Khafra 2520-2494
Menkaura 2490-2472

5th dynasty (2465-2323)
Userkaf 2465-2458
Sahura 2458-2446

6th dynasty (2323-2150)
Pepy I 2289-2255
Pepy II 2246-2152

First Intermediate Period
(2150-1994)

7th dynasty
Did not exist

8th dynasty (2150-2135)

*9th and 10th dynasties
(2135-2040)*

11th dynasty (2135-1994)
Mentuhotep II 2065-2014

Middle Kingdom (1994-1650)

12th dynasty (1994-1781)
Amenemhat I 1994-1964
Senusret I 1974-1929
Senusret II 1900-1881
Senusret III 1881-1842
Amenemhat III 1842-1794
Amenemhat IV 1798-1785

13th dynasty (1781-1650)
Uahibra-Hor

▼ *Statuary group depicting Rameses II,* Turin, Museo Egizio, C 767.

14th dynasty (1710-1650)

Second Intermediate Period (1650-1550)

15th and 16th dynasties (1650-1550)
Hyksos kings and governors

17th dynasty (1650-1550)

New Kingdom (1550-1075)

18th dynasty (1550-1291)
Amenhotep I 1525-1504
Thutmose I 1504-1492
Thutmose II 1492-1479
Hatshepsut 1479-1458
Thutmose III 1479-1425
Amenhotep II 1428-1397
Thutmose IV 1397-1387
Amenhotep III 1387-1350
Amenhotep IV/Akhenaten 1350-1333
Smenkhkara 1335-1333
Tutankhamun 1333-1323
Ay 1323-1319
Horemheb 1319-1291

19th dynasty (1291-1185)
Rameses I 1291-1289
Sety I 1289-1278
Rameses II 1279-1212
Merenptah 1212-1202

20th dynasty (1187-1075)
Sethnakhte 1187-1184
Rameses III 1184-1153

Third Intermediate Period (1075-664)

21st dynasty (1075-945)

22nd dynasty (945-718)
Osorkon I 924-899
Osorkon II 883-850

23rd dynasty (820-718)
Osorkon III 788-760

24th dynasty (730-712)

25th dynasty (775-653)
Piankhy (Piy) 745-713
Taharqo 690-664

Late Period (664-332)

26th dynasty (664-525)
Apries 589-570
Amasis 570-526

27th dynasty (525-404)
Cambyses II 525-522
Darius I 521-486

28th dynasty (404-399)

29th dynasty (399-380)

30th dynasty (380-342)
Nectanebo I 380-362
Nectanebo II 360-342

31st dynasty (342-332)

Ptolemaic Period (332-30)

The Macedonians (332-305)
Alexander the Great 332-323

Ptolemaic dynasty (305-30)
Ptolemy V Epiphanes 205-180

▲ *Statue of a Ptolemaic king,* Cairo, Egyptian Museum, CG 701.

Index of Names

Ahhotep, name of several princesses and queens during the 17th and 18th dynasties, p. 57.

Akhenaten, see Amenhotep IV.

Alexander the Great (356-323 BC), Macedonian commander who founded one of the greatest empires of the ancient world, pp. 122, 126.

Amasis, 26th-dynasty king, pp. 116-117.

Amenemhat I, vizier and then king, founder of the 12th dynasty, p. 48.

Amenemhat III, 12th-dynasty king, son of Senusret III, pp. 52-54.

Amenemhat IV, last king of the 12th dynasty, p. 52.

Amenhotep, son of Hapu, architect and vizier to Amenhotep III, built the king's city-palace on the west bank at Thebes, p. 73.

Amenhotep I, 18th-dynasty king, son and successor of Ahmose and Ahmose-Nefertari, p. 60.

Amenhotep II, 18th-dynasty king, son of Thutmose III, pp. 64-65.

Amenhotep III, 18th-dynasty king, son of Thutmose IV, pp. 67, 72-76, 78.

Amenhotep IV, 18th-dynasty king, son of Amenhotep III. In the third year of his reign, changed his name to Akhenaten ('He who is useful to Aten'), pp. 72, 76-83, 86-87, 91.

Ankhhaf, son of Sneferu, vizier under Khafra, tomb is at Giza, p. 25.

Ankhtyfy, ruled the 2nd and 3rd *nomes* of Upper Egypt during the First Intermediate Period, and conducted various military campaigns against neighbouring districts, p. 38.

Antef, chancellor and military commander under Mentuhotep II; his tomb is near the king's temple at Deir el-Bahri, p. 45.

Arsinoe II (316-270 BC), daughter of Ptolemy I, married her brother Ptolemy II, p. 127.

◀ *Seated statue of Harwa,* Cairo, Egyptian Museum, JE 37386.

Aset, 18th-dynasty queen, wife of Thutmose II and mother of Thutmose III, p. 64.

Ashayt, 11th-dynasty princess, daughter of Mentuhotep II. Her tomb is at Deir el-Bahri, beside her father's, p. 45.

Atet, wife of the architect Nefermaat, pp. 26-27.

Ay, priest who became king during the 18th dynasty, p 86

Bay, official during the time of Akhenaten, p. 83.

Belzoni, Giovanni Battista (1778-1823), Italian adventurer who went to Egypt and collected antiquities for the English consul Henry Salt. He was the first to enter the Great Temple at Abu Simbel and the pyramid of Khafra, and was responsible for the discovery of the tomb of Sety I in the Valley of the Kings, p. 142.

Cambyses II, Persian king. Defeated the Egyptians in 525 BC and annexed the Nile valley to the vast Achaemenid empire, p. 120.

Cyrus II, Persian king, p. 120.

Darius I, Persian king and 27th-dynasty pharaoh, pp. 120-121.

Djedefra, 4th-dynasty king, son of Khufu, p. 24.

◀ *Statue of Queen Nefertari* (detail), Luxor temple, Rameses II courtyard.

Index of Divinities

Ahura-Mazda, supreme divinity of Zoroastrianism, p. 120.

Amun, Amun-Ra, principal god of Thebes who became

▲ *Statue of the god Horus,* Temple of Edfu, courtyard.

▲ *The goddess Isis,* tomb of Horemheb (KV 57), Valley of the Kings.

increasingly important during the New Kingdom, and was eventually elevated to the role of a tutelary divinity in various parts of Egypt. He is represented as a man wearing a crown with two long plumes, pp. 46, 49, 62, 66, 78-80, 82, 86, 100, 102, 114, 121.

Anubis, male divinity with the head of a jackal, presided over the funerary cult and was believed to have invented the technique of mummification. He accompanied the dead person to the hereafter, and was therefore identified with Mercury during the Roman period, p. 114.

Aten, the solar disc, source of life and heat, began to be mentioned as a divinity under Amenhotep III. However, it was during the reign of Amenhotep IV-Akhenaten that his cult, mainly instituted to counter the authority of the priest-hood of Amun, was precisely codified and started to become widespread in Egypt. When Akhenaten died, the worship of Aten was suppressed, pp. 78-80, 86.

Atum, the primordial solar divinity, patron of Heliopolis, symbolized by the setting sun. He is represented as a man wearing a double crown, symbolizing his rule over the whole of Egypt, p. 87.

Hathor, the incarnation of the quintessence of

femininity, who was widely worshipped in many areas of Egypt. She is represented as a cow or as a woman with cow's ears, pp. 32, 63, 92, 100.

Hemen, falcon-shaped god, patron of Moalla. His main function was to harpoon the hippopotamus, the incarnation of evil, p. 113.

Horus, son of Osiris and Isis, often represented as a falcon or a falcon-headed man. He was worshipped in various parts of Egypt, and the reigning king was identified with him, pp. 92, 96, 100, 109, 128-129.

Isis, wife of Osiris and mother of Horus, widely worshipped throughout the Mediterranean in Roman times. During the pharaonic period, she was depicted as a woman with a throne, or a solar disc and two cow's horns, on her head, pp. 7, 90-91, 109, 115, 128-129.

Maat, goddess of justice and daughter of Ra, shown as a woman wearing an ostrich feather on her head. She represents the principle of order which inspires the king as he governs. The ostrich feather often also

◄ *Statue of the god Anubis from the treasure of Tutankhamun,* Cairo, Egyptian Museum, JE 61444.

Osiris, brother and husband of Isis, born of the union between the sky goddess Nut and the earth god Geb. Became king of Egypt and was then killed by his brother Seth. Was worshipped as king of the dead and represented as a mummy and with the *atef,* a white crown with two ostrich plumes. He was principally worshipped in the city of Abydos, pp. 92, 109, 114-115, 125.

Ptah, patron of Memphis and one of the tutelary divinities of Egypt, depicted as a mummy with the helmet typically worn by artisans, of whom he was also the protector, p. 100.

Ra, the sun god, worshipped mainly at Heliopolis. Shown as a man with the head of a falcon crowned with the solar disc, pp. 32, 67, 92, 96, 100.

Ra-Horakhty, divinity formed as a result of the assimilation of Ra and Horakhty, 'Horus of the horizons', pp. 92, 100.

Selqet, scorpion goddess, the protector of the king and the boat of the sun since the remotest antiquity. She is shown as a woman with a scorpion on her head, pp. 90-91.

Sobek, crocodile god, originated in Upper Egypt and was worshipped throughout the country but particularly at El-Fayum. Depicted as a man with a crocodile's head, pp. 72, 128.

Thoth, god of writing and associated with the moon. Represented as a man with the head of an ibis crowned with the solar disc. May also be shown as an ibis or baboon, pp. 103, 124.

Toeris, protecting god of childbirth and babies. He is shown as a combination of different animals: the mouth of a hippopotamus, the ears of a bull, the body and breasts of a pregnant woman, the tail of a crocodile and the paws of a lion, p. 117.

Wadjyt, the cobra goddess, symbolized Lower Egypt in conjunction with Nekhbet,

▼ *The god Ptah,* Valley of the Queens, tomb of Nefertari (QV 66).

the vulture goddess, who represented Upper Egypt. Wadjyt is shown as a woman with a red crown or as a cobra, pp. 91, 125.

appears as a counterweight to the dead person's heart on Anubis's weighing scales when the dead are judged.

Mut, wife of Amun, is represented as a woman wearing a double crown and with the head of a vulture. There was a temple dedicated exclusively to her near that of her divine husband at Karnak, p. 66.

Neith, goddess originating in Sais, often portrayed as a woman wearing the red crown of Lower Egypt and holding a bow and arrows.

Nekhbet, vulture goddess symbolizing Upper Egypt (in association with the cobra goddess Wadjyt, who represented Lower Egypt). She is depicted as a woman with a white crown, or as a vulture, pp. 91, 125.

Nephthys, sister and wife of Seth, was involved with her sister Isis in seeking and remaking the dismembered body of Osiris. Tutelary divinity of the 8th *nome* of Lower Egypt, and represented as a woman with her own name in hieroglyphs on her head, pp. 90-91.

APPENDICES

Egyptian Art around the World

EGYPT

Cairo, Egyptian Museum.
Ideally, any tour of the
world's leading museums
with collections of Egyptian
antiquities would have to
start in Egypt itself. The
Egyptian Museum in Cairo
has over 140,000 pharaonic
antiquities dating from the
most ancient times to the
Roman conquest. The first
nucleus of antiquities was
assembled in Cairo by
Auguste Mariette in the
mid-19th century, but the
current building was inaugurated in 1900. A tour of
the uniquely important
monuments on the ground
floor provides a
comprehensive overview of
Egyptian art from the predynastic period to the first
centuries of our era
(pp. 9, 15-16, 18, 20, 23-27,
31-34, 37, 39-43, 47, 49, 51,
53-55, 57, 60-63, 65, 73,
80-81, 83-84, 93, 96-97,

99, 102-103, 105, 108-109,
112, 117-119, 121).
The upper floor houses
smaller objects, jewels,
mummies and funerary
items, including the vast
treasure of Tutankhamun
(pp. 85, 90-91).

**Luxor, Museum of
Egyptian Art.** Contains over
100 masterpieces from the
countless finds made in the
region, which is one of the
world's richest
archaeological areas (pp. 65,
72-73, 77-78). One recently
added room contains the 25
sculptures found by chance
in the Luxor temple in 1989
(pp 74, 75, 85).

**Aswan, Museum of Nubian
Civilization.** This recently
opened museum contains a
number of masterpieces from
the period when Egypt was
governed by the 25th-
dynasty Kushite kings
(p. 112).

EUROPE

Turin, Museo Egizio.
Houses one of the most
distinguished Egyptian
collections in the world, and
was established using the
collection of the French
consul Bernardino Drovetti,
acquired in 1824 by the
state of Piedmont (pp. 12-
13, 21, 51). This contained a
number of impressive works
of sculpture, including the
famous *Statue of Rameses
II*, p. 98. The Egyptian
collection was later
significantly expanded
thanks to excavations by

▲ *Horemheb*,
Leiden, Rijksmuseum
van Oudheiden.

Ernesto Schiaparelli. These
led to the acquisition of
finds from particular periods
such as the First
Intermediate Period (pp. 38-
39), or geographical locations such as the village of
Deir el-Medina (p. 104).
Many objects not found
elsewhere make the Turin
collection very special.

Paris, Musée du Louvre.
The Louvre's Egyptian
collection was based on
Drovetti's second collection
and, most importantly, that
of the British consul Henry
Salt (pp. 8, 13, 15, 18, 21,
24, 50, 57, 75, 78, 83, 92,
104-105, 108-110, 112-113,
121). Further finds from the
numerous French
excavations in the Nile
valley were then added.
France's primary role in
excavating Nubian
monuments resulted in a
donation by the Egyptian
government of the upper
part of one of the *Colossal
statues of Amenhotep IV* in
his temple at Karnak (p. 81).

**London, The British
Museum.** The Rosetta Stone
entered this museum's
collection as part of the
spoils of war taken from the
French following the failure
of Napoleon's expedition to

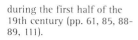
◀ The central gallery of the Egyptian Museum, Cairo.

Egypt. In the years immediately afterwards, the British consul Henry Salt donated and sold numerous antiquities which he had collected in Egypt. One of these was the *Colossal head of Rameses II* found by Belzoni among the ruins of Rameses' temple at Thebes (p. 99). Today, The British Museum has one of the richest Egyptian collections in the world, thanks particularly to the excavations of the Egypt Exploration Society, and many private donations (pp. 12-14, 16, 47, 60, 75).

Berlin, Ägyptisches Museum. The reign of Akhenaten, which is crucial for any understanding of Egyptian art, is documented by finds at the Egyptian Museum in Cairo and the Ägyptisches Museum in Berlin. These come from German excavations at Tell el-Amarna (pp. 79, 81-82, 84), and include the very famous *Head of Queen Nefertiti* (p. 84) which, decades after it was discovered, is still the subject of continual requests for its return by the Egyptian government. The Berlin collection, which was recently reunited after a long period of being divided between the two Germanys, also includes many fine written documents and works of art relating to all periods of pharaonic history (pp. 17, 35, 50, 53, 56, 72, 105, 109, 111, 116, 122, 126).

Leiden, Rijksmuseum van Oudheden. One of the richest collections of Egyptian art in Europe, based around a number of private collections acquired during the first half of the 19th century (pp. 61, 85, 88-89, 111).

Vienna, Kunsthistorisches Museum. Founded when Grand Duke Maximilian of Austria donated his Egyptian collection in the mid-19th century (pp. 31, 123).

Munich, Staatliche Sammlung Ägyptischer Kunst. Includes a series of masterpieces acquired on the antiquarian market over the past twenty years (pp. 17, 44).

St Petersburg, Hermitage. Russia's most important collection of Egyptian finds (p. 127).

UNITED STATES

New York, The Metropolitan Museum of Art. Owns one of the most important Egyptian collections in the world, based on generous donations by individuals and finds from Herbert E. Winlock's excavations in Egypt during the early 20th century (pp. 33, 52, 73, 94-95, 122, 127).

New York, Brooklyn Museum. This collection also derives from donations by individuals of pieces of great historical and artistic value (pp. 35-37, 117, 127).

Boston, Museum of Fine Arts. Another collection of great importance for our knowledge of Egyptian art; its particular strength is the collection amassed by George A. Reisner during his many excavations at Giza and in Sudan (pp. 25, 30-32).

▲ Statues in the Museo Egizio, Turin.

To Sergio Donadoni,
my teacher

Published in cooperation with
La Biblioteca editrice s.r.l., Milan

© 1999 by Leonardo Arte s.r.l., Milan
Elemond Editori Associati
All rights reserved

First published in Great Britain in 2002
by The British Museum Press
A division of The British Museum Company Ltd
46 Bloomsbury Street, London WC1B 3QQ

A catalogue record for this book is available from the
British Library.

ISBN 0 7141 1950 4

Printed and bound in Italy.

Series editors: Stefano Peccatori and Stefano Zuffi

Text by Francesco Tiradritti
English translation by Phil Goddard in association with
First Edition Translations Ltd, Cambridge, UK
English text design and cover by Martin Richards

Photographic credits:
Sergio Anelli, Milan
Archivio Electa, Milan
Archivio Patrizia Piacentini, Milan
Archivio Francesco Tiradritti, Montepulciano (Siena)
Araldo De Luca, Rome - White Star
Giacomo Lovera, Settimo Torinese (Turin)
Studio Margil, Milan

We are grateful to the museums and archives which have
been kind enough to supply photographs. Please notify
the publisher of any illustrations which have not been
properly credited.